D0045266

The
New
CAPITALIST
MANIFESTO

The
New
CAPITALIST
MANIFESTO

building a disruptively better business

Umair Haque

HARVARD BUSINESS REVIEW PRESS

Boston, Massachusetts

Copyright 2011 Umair Haque
The foreword is © 2011 Gary Hamel
All rights reserved

Printed in the United States of America

11 10 9 8 7 6 5 4 3

No part of this publication may be reproduced, stored in or introduced into a retrieval system, or transmitted, in any form, or by any means (electronic, mechanical, photocopying, recording, or otherwise), without the prior permission of the publisher. Requests for permission should be directed to permissions@hbsp.harvard.edu, or mailed to Permissions, Harvard Business School Publishing, 60 Harvard Way, Boston, Massachusetts 02163.

Library of Congress Cataloging-in-Publication Data

Haque, Umair.
    The new capitalist manifesto : building a disruptively better business / Umair Haque.
      p. cm.
    ISBN 978-1-4221-5858-6 (hbk. : alk. paper)   1. Capitalism—Social aspects.   2. Economic development—Social aspects.   3. Value.   4. Organizational effectiveness.   5. Strategic planning—Social aspects.   6. Social responsibility of business.   I. Title.
    HB501.H347 2011
    330.12'2—dc22   2010027957

The paper used in this publication meets the requirements of the American National Standard for Permanence of Paper for Publications and Documents in Libraries and Archives Z39.48-1992.

This book is dedicated with gratitude to
Dr. Nadeem ul Haque, Farida Haque, and Ikram ul Haque
for having the courage to take an improbable journey,
the conviction to create the future,
and the wisdom to teach me why.

Contents

Contents

Foreword

Capitalism is dead. Long live capitalism.

I'm a capitalist by conviction and by profession. I believe the best economic system is one that rewards entrepreneurship and risk taking, maximizes customer choice, uses markets to allocate scarce resources, and minimizes the regulatory burden on business. If there's a better recipe for creating prosperity, I haven't seen it—and neither have you.

So why does capitalism have a major image problem? Why do the majority of consumers in the developed world doubt that large corporations are good for society? Why are executives regarded as ethically inferior to journalists and even lawyers? Why are CEOs more likely to be portrayed as villains than heroes in the popular media? Why do people seem to *expect* big companies to behave badly—to ravish the environment, exploit employees, and mislead customers?

Some blame Wall Street for this state of affairs. In March 2009, the *Financial Times* claimed that the "credit crisis had destroyed faith in the free market ideology that has dominated Western thinking for a decade."[1] As central bankers struggled to contain the subprime contagion, some wondered whether capitalism would survive the crisis. At a minimum, argued a chorus of jaundiced journalists and grandstanding politicians, a new form of capitalism was needed—one in which executives would bow to the state and magisterial policy makers would rein in the excesses of the market.

While one should never underestimate the ability of risk-besotted financiers to wreak havoc, the real threat to capitalism isn't unfettered financial cunning. It is, instead, the inability (or unwillingness) of executives to confront the changing expectations of their stakeholders about the role of business in society. In recent years, consumers and citizens have become increasingly disgruntled with the implicit contract that governs the rights and obligations of society's most powerful economic actors—large industrial companies. To many, this contract seems one-sided—it has worked well for CEOs and shareholders, but not so well for everyone else.

You don't have to read *Adbusters* or be a paid-up member of Greenpeace to wonder whose interests are really being served by big business. When it comes to "free markets," there's plenty to be cynical about: the food industry's long and illicit love affair with trans fats, Merck's dissembling about the risks of Vioxx, Facebook's apparently cavalier attitude toward consumer privacy, BP's shocking disregard for the environment, and the everyday reality of grossly exaggerated product claims and buck-passing customer "service" agents.

If individuals around the world have lost faith in business, it's because business has, in many ways, betrayed that trust. In this sense, the threat to capitalism (and capitalists) is both more prosaic and more profound than that posed by over-leveraged bankers—more prosaic in that the danger comes not from the wild schemes of rocket scientists but from the slowly accreting frustrations and anxieties of ordinary folks; and more profound in the sense that the problem is truly existential—it reflects a fundamental divergence of world views and therefore can neither be solved nor thwarted by political lobbying or feel-good advertising.

Make no mistake, though: capitalism has no challengers. Like democracy, it's the worst sort of system except for all the others—and that's exactly why we all have a stake in making it better. If we fail to do so, the growing discontent with business's myopic view of its accountabilities will embolden all those who believe CEOs should answer to those who are eager to replace the invisible hand of the market with the iron hand of the state.

This is not an outcome, I think, that most of us would welcome. While cinching the regulatory straitjacket even tighter might protect us from capitalism's worst excesses, it would also rob us of its bounties. So we must hope that executives will face up to the fact that an irreversible revolution in expectations is under way.

I believe that millions of consumers and citizens are already convinced of a fact that many executives are still reluctant to admit: the legacy model of economic production that has driven the "modern" economy forward over the last hundred years is on its last legs. Like a piece of clapped-out equipment, it's held together with bailing wire and duct tape, is grossly inefficient, and spews out clouds of noxious fumes.

While we're all grateful that someone invented this clattering, savage machine a century and more ago, we'll also be happy when it finally gets carted off to the scrap yard and is replaced with something a bit less menacing.

We know the future cannot be an extrapolation of the past. As the great-grandchildren of the industrial revolution, we have learned at last that the heedless pursuit of more is unsustainable and, ultimately, unfulfilling. Our planet, our security, our sense of equanimity, and our very souls demand something better, something different.

So we long for a kinder, gentler sort of capitalism—one that views us as more than mere "consumers," one that understands the difference between maximizing consumption and maximizing quality of life, one that doesn't sacrifice the future for the present, one that regards our planet as sacred, and one that narrows rather than exploits the inequalities in the world.

So what stands in the way of creating a conscientious, accountable, and sustainable sort of capitalism—a system that in the long-term is actually habitable?

It is, I think, a matrix of deeply held beliefs about what business is actually *for*, about who it serves and how it creates value. Many of these beliefs are near-canonical—at least among those who've been to business school or have spent a few decades inside a Global 1000 company. Nevertheless, we have reached a point in the history of business where even fundamental tenets must be reexamined.

Among the beliefs that most descrve to be challenged:

- The paramount objective of a business is to make money (rather than to enhance human well-being in economically efficient ways).

- Corporate leaders can reasonably be held accountable only for the immediate effects of their actions (and not for the second- and third-order consequences of their single-minded pursuit of growth and profitability).

- Executives should be evaluated and compensated on the basis of short-term earnings performance (rather than long-term value creation).

- A "brand" is something that is built with marketing dollars (rather than something that is socially constructed by all of the firm's constituents).

- The firm's "customers" are the people who buy its products (rather than all those who are influenced by its actions).

- It's legitimate for a company to profit by exploiting customer ignorance or constraining customer choice.

- Customers care only about how a product performs and how much it costs (and not about the values that were honored or defiled in the making and selling of that product).

- Customers are end users (rather than full partners in the work of value-creation and value-sharing).

- Customers who've been ignored, manipulated, locked in, duped, or lied to will nurse their anger in private (rather than join forces with fellow sufferers to publicly shame their persecutors).

- A company can successfully use its market power and political leverage to obstruct a disruptive technology or stymie a new and unconventional competitor.

- Employees are human resources first and human beings second.

- Business is about advantage, focus, differentiation, superiority, and excellence (and not about love, joy, honor, beauty, and justice).

These beliefs are the *real* threat to capitalism. They are narcissistic and self-indulgent—and have grown even less attractive and defensible in the fifty-seven years since General Motors' then-chairman, Charles Wilson, proclaimed that "what was good for GM was good for America."

I may be an ardent supporter of capitalism—but I also understand that while individuals have inalienable, God-given rights, corporations do not. Society can demand of corporations what it wills. Of course, as consumers and citizens, we must be wise enough to realize that companies cannot remedy every social ill or deliver every social benefit, and we must also acknowledge the fact that a regulatory regime that would insulate us from all of capitalism's vices would also deny us its virtues.

Nevertheless, executives need to understand that today they face the same hard choice that confronts every teenager—drive responsibly or lose your license.

This is the starting premise of the book you now hold in your hands. But in *The New Capitalist Manifesto*, Umair Haque goes farther—much farther. He outlines the new beliefs that must replace the shortsighted and self-limiting assumptions of the industrial age. He draws a host of invaluable lessons from companies that have already embraced the challenge of reinventing capitalism. With fervor and wit he makes an unimpeachable case that it is possible for a business to thrive socially *and* financially in the new age of accountability. This book is more than a manifesto, it's a blueprint for building the sort of twenty-first-century company that will be loved by its customers, envied by its peers, and admired by all those who care about the future of our planet.

Gary Hamel

Preface

In 1776, one man found himself at the center of a maelstrom. Hurricanes of change lashed the globe: growing markets, expanding international trade, a rising middle class, disruptive technologies, novel commercial entities. Yet, where his contemporaries saw chaos, Adam Smith saw hitherto unimagined possibilities.

In *The Wealth of Nations*, Smith envisioned with startling prescience a very different prosperity: one in which *capitalists*, not the mercantilists, aristocrats, and agrarians who had preceded them, held sway. Stop for a moment to consider the keenness of that insight. In 1776, horses provided power for carts and carriages. Steam-powered locomotives would not arrive until the next century. The economy's central axis was households, not even medium-sized corporations. Ownership of land, mills, tools, and rights was sharply concentrated in the hands of the nobility, and passed down through the patrician generations. "Joint-stock companies," still new forms, required government charter or royal decree for incorporation and, until around 1850, had liability unlimited enough to land an unfortunate shareholder in debtors' prison. The overwhelming balance of organizational power was still held by sprawling, storied guilds, like the City of London's Worshipful Company of Ironmongers (or carpenters or cooks or mercers, to name just four). And the ruling dogma of protectionism saw laissez-faire thinking as alarmingly, dangerously avant-garde.

It was, in short, *not* a world in which the capitalist enterprise as we know it today might have been foreseen to flourish. Yet, by seeing through the maelstrom, Smith synthesized, in detail and with ruthless logic, his new vision of prosperity. Though many similar tomes followed, Smith's masterpiece remains the original capitalist manifesto, the founding document of industrial era prosperity.

I'd like to pose a question: what if the future of capitalism will be *as different* from its present as Adam Smith's vision was from *its* present? What if twenty-first-century prosperity differs from industrial era prosperity as radically as *it* did from its now seemingly prehistoric predecessor? Consider, for a moment, the striking parallels between Smith's maelstrom and ours. Globally, the Internet has given rise to hyperconnection. The nations formerly known as the third world have become a rising, roaring middle. Nascent technologies like cleantech and nanotech hint at hitherto unimagined possibilities. The "corporation" is mitotically dividing into many different kinds of commercial entities, whether social businesses, hedge funds, or "for benefit" corporations. Today, as then, the world is shedding yesterday's skin.

I'm no Adam Smith, but I'd like to invite you to take a voyage with me. It's a journey of imagination, where we'll envisage production, consumption, and exchange through new eyes. It's an expedition on which we'll explore the zephyrs and siroccos that are reshaping profitability, performance, and advantage. And it's a quest for insight into how commerce, finance, and trade might—just might—be transformed, and, more vitally, become *transformative*. Let's stride boldly, as Adam Smith did, past the horizon of commerce, finance, and trade as we know them, venture off the map of industrial era capitalism—and explore the uncharted *terra nova* of tomorrow's prosperity.

Why should you join me? Consider the following story. In 1494, a Franciscan friar published an unlikely blockbuster. Despite its awkward mouthful of a title, *Everything About Arithmetic, Geometry and Proportion* flew hot and fast off the Gutenberg presses. Describing the way Venetian merchants kept their books in order, Luca Pacioli formalized what we know today as double-entry bookkeeping—where every transaction is booked simultaneously in two different accounts so that debits match credits. Fast forward: in 1994, sustainability trailblazer John Elkington coined the term "triple bottom line" for an accounting system that booked transactions in financial terms as well as social and environmental ones. Half a millennium, *five hundred* long years, passed between the birth of accounting—and the first glimmering seeds of its rebirth.

Preface

Consider the steady breakthrough after breakthrough in every sphere of life. Jonas Salk's polio vaccine, the Green Revolution of the 1960s, the transistor, and, of course, the Internet, to name just a few. But most of the *cornerstones* of capitalism have changed at a snail's pace, if at all. In fact, they predate Adam Smith, whose genius wasn't to *invent* them but, for the first time, to weave together the strands of their bigger story. The assembly line—today, called a value chain—was pioneered by Britain's first industrialists in the eighteenth century. Shareholder value, sanctified in the 1980s by academics, is a clever spin on the eighteenth century's rising joint-stock corporations. The corporation itself was born during the seventeenth century's great age of exploration. Like the five-hundred-year gap between double entries and triple bottom lines, new cornerstones are rarely laid. Is it any wonder then that so many companies (and economies) are struggling to keep pace with the twenty-first-century's challenges?

Just as Giza's pyramids have crumbled over the centuries, so cornerstones aren't eternal and everlasting. It's not too hard to see, for example, why an institution invented in the fifteenth century to keep the books of a handful of silk and spice merchants in order might not be the most accurate way to keep the global economy's books in the twenty-first. Vicious volatility, deepening scarcity, activist shareholders, power shifting to the people formerly known as *consumers:* they're just a few of the new challenges testing yesterday's titans—whether companies, countries, or people—and finding them wanting, revealing the drawbacks of cornerstones built in and for very different eras. Today, the tectonic plates are shifting, and yesterday's weathered, worn cornerstones are beginning to crack.

You wouldn't run your trading floor on terminals from 1980. You wouldn't ask your distribution fleet to use engines from 1950. And you probably wouldn't use carrier pigeons to convey vital knowledge to your headquarters. Why then are companies, countries, and the global economy still anchored atop musty, tottering cornerstones? Because building *new* ones is an art in its infancy. This book isn't just the chronicle of a new crop of world-builders. More deeply, it's a *guide* to crafting the new cornerstones they're learning to chisel.

My goal is to help you become a bellwether of twenty-first-century capitalism, a master stonemason of new cornerstones, which, when sunk in today's economic soil, yield strong, thick, long-lasting foundations. I'll argue that *institutional innovation,* the art of carving them, is the key to building a higher level of advantage. I'll sketch a blueprint you can use to conceive of—and then, if you wish, to *construct*—structures set on new cornerstones, that can yield not just more, but more powerful value.

That's what this book is—and here's what this book *isn't.* Michelangelo, when asked his secret, answered: "Every block of stone has a statue inside it, and it is the task of the sculptor to discover it." I can be a guide, mentor, and counselor, but I can't discover what's inside *your* stone. Though the pages that follow are filled with examples, this isn't a call to go forth and imitate. I don't want you to follow an example, but to *be* the example. My ambition is that you understand *why* innovators are carving new stones, *what* they gain from them, *how* each works—and then find the statue in *your* stone. My insight matters less than your vision, ambition, and passion. So think of this book not as a laundry list, but a toolkit. I can give you the chisel, hammer, wedge, and brush, but only *you* can be the sculptor.

Here then is the lens through which I'll ask you to discover the statue inside *your* stone. A capitalism where companies, countries, and economies reach a higher apex of advantage—one where bigger purpose rouses untapped human potential of every employee, customer, and future customer, instead of deadening it. One where fiercer passion makes innovation as natural as drawing breath, spontaneously combusting the spark of creativity instead of dousing its flame with lowest common denominators. One where deeper meaning replaces the drab grind of repetition with challenging and compelling work that elevates the soul. Where more authentic power flows from shared principles instead of (yawn) sweeter carrots and heftier sticks. Where greater resourcefulness means being not the natural world's conqueror, but its champion. Where higher-quality value is created by doing stuff of greater *worth*. And, ultimately, where companies compete not just to change the rules, but to change the world. These aren't, of course, the idle dreams of stargazers. They're the motive power of prosperity—the only resolutions to the relentless, lethal challenges bearing swiftly down on countries, companies, and economies. For that reason, they *are* the engines of twenty-first-century advantage.

This, then, is a handbook for idealists and pragmatists, for revolutionaries and hard-boiled realists. If you're happy with the status quo, satisfied with the state of play, delighted by the incremental—put this book back on the shelf. If, on the other hand, you're dissatisfied with the status quo, if you wonder about the ballgame of business as usual, if you've begun to see a gap between what capitalism has been—and what it *can and should* be—then this book is for you, not just to read, but to use.

Acknowledgments

The book you're holding is really the result of contributions by many people—all of whom I'm deeply grateful to. I'm indebted to Gary Hamel, who helped me to better understand the art and science of management, for his invaluable counsel, his irreplaceable wisdom, and for inspiring me to embark on this journey. I owe a substantial debt to John Hagel III for his sage advice, steadfast encouragement, and for galvanizing me to see deeper and think bigger. It has been an exceptional privilege—and a great boon—for this green shoot to grow in the company of such mighty oaks. If there are any tiny morsels of merit in this book, they stand, in every way, on the far broader shoulders of these guides.

A warm thank you is also due to Hernán Sánchez Neira, CEO of Havas Media Intelligence, Alfonso Rodés Vilà, CEO of Havas Media, and Fernando Rodés Vilà, CEO of Havas,

Acknowledgments

for giving me every author's most precious gift: the time to invest in writing. Their unflagging enthusiasm and support is what made this book possible.

I also drew on my conversations with the late Sumantra Ghoshal, the late Paul Geroski, Paddy Barwise, Julian Birkinshaw, Jeff Jarvis, Rishi Shahdadpuri, Chris Anderson, and Fred Wilson—as well as the groundbreaking research and insight of Richard Florida, Bill Easterly, Amartya Sen, Archon Fung, Joseph Stiglitz, Daron Acemoglu, Richard Easterlin, Richard Layard, Clayton Christensen, Michael Porter, Rosabeth Moss Kanter, Tom Peters, Charles Handy, and the late C.K. Prahalad. All were catalysts in enlarging my own inconsequential reflections.

Finally, I'm grateful to Adi Ignatius of the Harvard Business Review Group for giving me—the unlikeliest of novice authors—the chance and the privilege to work with the superlative team there. When it comes to the theory and practice of business, it's hard to think of another lineup of individuals so devoted to—and expert at—advancing the state of the art. In particular, I'm indebted to Eric Hellweg for giving me the room to develop the thoughts summarized here, often inelegantly, impetuously, and messily, at my hbr.org blog. And last, but quite the opposite of least, I'm in editor extraordinaire Sarah Green's debt. She was a partner on every step of this journey, and without her boundless energy, unflappable enthusiasm, lucid criticism, and incisive suggestions, this book would surely have been just a dim shadow of what it is.

Acknowledgments

If this book has any worth, the merit lies with these peo-ple. The many imperfections and limitations it surely has—for which I might ask you to forgive me in advance—can be readily assigned to me.

Umair Haque

July 2010

Chapter One

The Blueprint of
a Better Kind
of Business

HAT DO YOU see when you look at the future of capitalism? When you look one, two, or three decades forward, what's different about prosperity? Which *kinds* of capital will be new, unorthodox, unexplored—and disruptively valuable? What will be the state of the art in defining, measuring, monitoring, and managing human achievement and the wealth it creates? To outperform in terms of newer, better, broader conceptions of affluence, what will tomorrow's marketplace virtuosos maximize and minimize? To make it happen, how will they utilize, allocate, and renew capital differently? And what mind-set, ethos, and character will

distinguish successful companies, countries, and economies from struggling ones?

To glean more foresight, here are some curious facts that might strike you if you looked closely at preeminent capitalists today. You might notice the world's biggest company striving only to sell products that benefit the environment—and then not just asking, but actively *empowering* activists and visionaries to ensure that it does so. You might glimpse the world's best-known maker of cutting-edge athletic gear designing recyclable shoes and then, instead of marketing them by spending big bucks on "celeb-vertising," simply helping everyone who buys them learn to get the most out of them. You might spy the world's most powerful media company displaying *no* ads on the world's most valuable media property. You might see one of the world's most historic consumer goods companies beginning to turn itself inside out: to help transform the people formerly known as *consumers* into *producers*. And you might behold yesterday's herd of tired, lumbering giants—even as their herd is being mercilessly culled—*continuing* to pretend that business as usual is good enough, despite their razor-thin margins getting thinner every year.

If you look closely and patiently enough, you might not discern full-blown revolution (as in "the successful overthrow of authority")—*yet*. But I'd wager that you'd at least detect, in vivid detail, its prelude—rebellion, or open resistance to, and fierce defiance of, the precepts and doctrines of yesterday's dogma. Examining it carefully, you might see what I see: the first tiny shoots of what scholar Thomas

Kuhn called a *paradigm shift*—not a small step, but a giant leap from one system of thought to its successor, which recasts an art or science in a radical new light.

Today, a new generation of renegades—companies as seemingly different as Walmart, Nike, Google, and Unilever, for example—are thriving not in spite of but *by* rebelling against the tired, toxic orthodoxies of industrial age capitalism. Their secret? Haltingly, imperfectly, often messily, never easily, they're learning to become twenty-first-century capitalists. Maybe, just maybe, call it economic enlightenment: today's radical innovators are vanguards, voyaging past the edge of the drab, lackluster world of business as usual—and exploring a terra incognita rich with possibility, where higher peaks of prosperity, built on stronger, thicker bedrock, can be glimpsed.

The story I want to share with you isn't just about companies. At the root, it's about *cornerstones:* how, as the anchors of companies, countries, and economies, they are the foundations of plenitude—or of penury. Just as the Enlightenment culminated in new cornerstones for work, life, and play—like free markets, rational thinking, and the scientific method, to name just a few—so today's economic enlightenment is culminating in new cornerstones for production, consumption, and exchange, like *value cycles, value conversations,* and *betters.*

The story, though, is only half of my agenda. The *destination* I want to guide you to is a new blueprint. The new cornerstones at its heart are what promise to revolutionize a rusting, fading industrial era: they reimagine profitability,

reconceive value creation, and refresh advantage, toppling the centuries-old status quo of business *has* been, *can* be, and *should* be. Because they hold the possibility to heal, repair, and right—never completely, sometimes sparingly, but always *conceivably*—the age-old shortcomings, deficiencies, and flaws of capitalism, *while* strengthening its already formidable power to intensify the pace, magnitude, and potential of human accomplishment, their bedrock is deep-rooted, thick-set, and steadfastly unshakable. On their shoulders, the future foundations of prosperity rest.

. . .

Enlightenment is a word that shouldn't be used lightly. Here's my considered case for choosing it. The unvarnished truth is that capitalism is past its prime. It's an aging paradigm that has hit the point of maturity. It was built in an industrial age, and the rust and damage on its weathered iron and battered rivets are beginning to show.

You might not know that, examined carefully, growth in developed countries reached an inflection point decades ago, a negative one. It has been steadily slowing for the last half-*century.* This is no mere passing episode, but a lasting, historic shift more significant than a crisis, correction, or crash. Boardrooms are used to responding to microeconomic threats—new competitors, shocks in supply and demand, more complex markets. But today's biggest threat is of a different order. It's glaring down from the macroeconomic heights: prosperity itself has reached sharply diminishing returns.

Yesterday's industrial era model of growth is on its last tired legs today. There isn't much room to give until we approach the boundary where growth diminishes to the level of consumption just necessary to maintain today's standard of living, instead of enhancing it. If you look carefully, you might see the spark lighting the economic enlightenment's fuse: the global economy is reaching a decisive, defining moment. What powered prosperity in the twentieth century won't—and can't—power prosperity in the twenty-first.

You might say, wait, growth in GDP is just an increase in "product," and that's a flawed measure of prosperity. And you'd be right. The economist who created the very concept of GNP (now superceded by GDP), Nobel Laureate Simon Kuznets, warned, "The welfare of a nation can . . . scarcely be inferred from a measure of national income."[1] As I'll discuss, more meaningful, accurate measures of welfare—how well people, communities, and society fare—have stagnated, while GDP has grown. Conversely, you might ask, what about developing countries? You'd be right again. Though they can aim for industrial era growth—despite all that's now apparent about its shortcomings—it has a hungry maw, and there isn't enough oil, copper, credit, employment, or export demand in the world for every nation to continue achieving prosperity that way. Doing so quickly deteriorates into a zero-sum game of beggar-thy-neighbor, where growth in some countries is counterbalanced by stagnation in others.

Yet, *even* in terms of its own flawed, central measure of success—growth—capitalism needs a reboot. This isn't to

disparage the great achievements of industrial age capitalism—-but to praise them. The greatest powerhouse of abundance the world has ever seen led to an explosive rise in income and living standards for vast swaths of the world's population. But that was yesterday. Today, perhaps it is yesterday's very triumphs that lay capitalism's decline bare. Here's what I gently suggest is the quandary: industrial age prosperity can advance only under a narrow set of conditions, all increasingly detached from today's economic reality.

The Great Imbalance

Here's an allegory in miniature. Imagine two worlds: The first is a *big* world of abundant resources and raw materials, an *empty* world where demand is infrequent and easily satiated, and a *stable* world where disasters are infrequent and weak. The second is a *tiny* world, emptying of raw resources, a *crowded* world where demand is always hungry, and a *fragile* world, where contagion of every kind can flow across the globe in a matter of minutes, days, or weeks. A big, empty, stable world is like a vast, placid, untouched game reserve. But a tiny, crowded, and fragile world is like an *ark*. Industrial era capitalism was built for a big, empty, stable world. But at the dawn of the twenty-first century, the world is more like an ark—tiny, fragile, and crowded.

Consuming, borrowing, and utilizing are the engines of prosperity in a big, empty, stable world, but the engines of crisis in a tiny, fragile, and crowded one. The three defining characteristics of what I call the industrial era's "dumb" growth, the last several decades have been their culmination. They've been an era of growth driven by the global *poor subsidizing the rich* to fuel the *overconsumption* of an array of more and more ephemeral goods and services dependent on steeply *diminishing returns economics,* where the natural world, communities, and society are marginalized. The developed world's largest creditors aren't other developed countries, but developing countries like China and oil-exporting nations like Nigeria.[2] What the developed world has plowed money into isn't innovation or investment, but raw, transient, consumption. The result? Tremendous and tremendously unsustainable global macroeconomic imbalances.

Dumb growth is locally, globally, and economically unsustainable. And because it is visibly failing to create a shared prosperity, corporations, investors, and entrepreneurs can no longer prosper merely by achieving it. In terms of *what* prosperity means, *how long* prosperity endures, to *whom* prosperity accrues, and *how* prosperity happens, the dumb growth of the twentieth century has had its day.

That's what the global economy discovered—the hard way. A long list of eminent thinkers has referred to the historic crisis of the noughties as "great" in many ways. Economic historian Niall Ferguson has called it a "Great Repression"; Harvard economist Kenneth Rogoff, a "Great Contraction"; Berkeley's Robert Reich, a "Great Crash."[3] When you think about it, what was great about it ultimately wasn't just its

7

magnitude. It was that the very foundations of economics were shaken by it.

Paul Samuelson, one of the grandfathers of macroeconomics, the first American to win the Nobel Prize in Economics, observed that "today we see how utterly mistaken was the Milton Friedman notion that a market system can regulate itself."[4] Alan Greenspan—a disciple of Friedman—admitted that he was "deeply dismayed" that "all of the sophisticated mathematics and computer wizardry" wasn't enough to make up for a systemic failure of "enlightened self-interest," and then noted that "the whole intellectual edifice" of financial economics "collapsed in the summer of [2008]." Barack Obama's top economic adviser and former president of Harvard, Larry Summers, said, "Large swaths of economics are going to have to be rethought on the basis of what's happened."[5]

In the 2009 Lionel Robbins Lectures at the London School of Economics (LSE), Nobel Laureate Paul Krugman argued that modern macroeconomics was "spectacularly useless at best, and positively harmful at worst." Willem Buiter, the eminent LSE economist, suggested that the last thirty years of economic training have been a "costly waste of time and other resources," driven by "aesthetic puzzles . . . rather than by a powerful desire to understand how the economy works." Another Nobel Laureate—Columbia University's renowned Joseph Stiglitz, who predicted the 2008 crash in 2006—concluded that "the debate over 'market fundamentalism,' the notion that unfettered markets, all by themselves, can ensure economic prosperity and growth," was "over." And

Treasury Secretary Tim Geithner has noted that tomorrow "capitalism will be different."[6]

Yet, there's little revolutionary about any of that. It would be hubris to presume we've reached the end of capitalism and found the perfect prescription for eternal, unbounded prosperity. Just as in any other socially built, culturally bound, human-run system, there's always room for improvement. That lesson is, I humbly suggest, the legacy of the great crisis of the noughties.

So how *could* we improve capitalism, if we were to try? What Greenspan, Samuelson, Krugman, and Stiglitz are referencing is the *institutions* of industrial era capitalism. Once thought to be the bedrock of prosperity, they turned out to be its quicksand: they are what went haywire, misallocating trillions in wealth. Nobel Laureate Douglass North, who won the prize for his pioneering work on institutions, defined them as "the humanly devised constraints that shape interaction." Daron Acemoglu, the eminent MIT economist, picks out an even more precise phrase from North about institutions: "In consequence, they structure incentives in human exchange, whether political, social, or economic."[7] Institutions are, in other words, the deep, underlying *cornerstones* of every social, political, or economic system. Economic institutions—those we are concerned with—order and organize production, consumption, and exchange. Industrial era capitalism can be thought of as just *one* possible set of institutional cornerstones.

Since 2005, I'd been discussing the likelihood of a great crisis—predicting no mere ephemeral crash, but a jagged,

historic tear in the global economy. Spurred on by the great crisis, inspired by North, Acemoglu, and scholars like Oliver E. Williamson and Elinor Ostrom, who jointly won the 2009 economics Nobel for pioneering the field of institutional economics, my team and I began a two-year long research program, asking two questions. *Were there renegades who, not contented with the cornerstones of industrial age capitalism, were rebelling against them? If so, how did they fare against their more traditionally minded rivals?*

Of course, there's no single, simple definition of capitalism. Rather, different perspectives—from the great Alfred Chandler's notion of managerial capitalism to Hyman Minsky's concept of financial capitalism to Joseph Schumpeter's idea of entrepreneurial capitalism—have emphasized different facets of a larger stone.[8] So first, we went back in time, combing through hundreds of articles, papers, and entries about capitalism in numerous reference works, journal articles, and books, seeking elegance: the *smallest* number of cornerstones or key institutions that would capture capitalism's essential features and characteristics. That handful of cornerstones is what our definition of industrial age capitalism is, at root.

The five cornerstones we ultimately distilled are so familiar to CEOs and clerks alike that they are invisible fixtures of everyday economic life: *value chains* as the means of production, *value propositions* as the means of positioning, *strategy* as the means of competition, *protecting marketplaces* as the means of advantage, and inert, fixed *goods* as the means of consumption. That's our institutional definition of twentieth-century capitalism: five foundational cornerstones that order, organize, and manage production and consumption. Now they aren't the only ones or an exhaustive list. Rather, they are those that we felt best synthesized the numerous, often conflicting definitions of capitalism.

Here's the flaw at their heart. Twentieth-century capitalism's cornerstones *shift costs to* and *borrow benefits from* people, communities, society, the natural world, or future generations. Both cost shifting and benefit borrowing are forms of economic harm that are unfair, nonconsensual, and often irreversible. Call it a great imbalance: not a transient *event*, like the "Great [insert ominous synonym here]," but an ongoing *relationship*, a titanic glitch in the global economy's vast scales. You can think of the great imbalance this way: industrial era capitalism's cornerstones undercount costs (ignoring many flavors of loss and damage) and overcount benefits (overstating how much products and services make people durably, tangibly, and meaningfully better off).

To illustrate, consider two industries usually found at opposite ends of town: banking and burger making. During the great housing bubble of the noughties, investment banks, hedge funds, and mortgage brokers sought to borrow benefits from each other by hiding assets in what New York University professor Nouriel Roubini has called a "shadow banking system," obtaining greater leverage by hiding assets from the next guy.[9] And, of course, they sought to shift costs to each other. Yves Smith, author of *ECONned* and the Naked Capitalism blog, has documented how toxic loans, like the aptly named NINJA ("No income, no job, no assets"), became business as usual in the financial industry, passed like

a hot potato from one party to next. The result? When the music stopped, a catastrophic breakdown of trust in counterparties paralyzed borrowers and lenders and caused the near collapse of global finance. Ultimately, costs were shifted to people, communities, society, and future generations, in a historic, unprecedented bailout. In 2010, reversing decades of allegiance to laissez-faire dogma, the International Monetary Fund proposed an international banking tax, equivalent to the expected value of the hidden costs and borrowed benefits of *tomorrow's* bailouts.

Collateralized debt obligations (CDOs) are the financial equivalent of fast-food burgers: both are mixtures of toxic mystery meat. How much does a burger *really* cost? You pay perhaps $3, but according to my back-of-the-envelope analysis, the authentic economic cost may be closer to $30. Environmental and health-care costs of as much as $10 are shifted to society and future generations. And benefits are borrowed from people, communities, and society: the beef, water, land, and even jobs that go into burgers are subsidized by as much as $20. If, for example, water were no longer subsidized in the Great Plains states, a pound of ground beef would cost $35, estimates James E. McWilliams, a fellow in Agrarian Studies at Yale University.[10] I don't mean to deny the mouth-watering temptation of a fresh, juicy burger. Rather, my point's about the stubborn reality of creating value: the $27 gap between the $3 or less the average American pays and the $30 or so a burger actually costs is economic harm that is done by industrial era food producers to people, communities, society, the natural world, and future generations. Using industrial era capitalism's cornerstones, costs can be shifted and benefits borrowed not merely by pennies, but by ten times—unseen harm of an order of magnitude.

Now I don't pretend those numbers are perfectly correct, down to the penny. The principle is what I'd like you to consider and delve into with me. It's possible to do similar calculations for oil, for instance, where the International Center for Technology Assessment has estimated that netting out hidden costs would add $4 per gallon to its price.[11] That imbalance—present in every industry under the sun— is the new economic calculus companies and countries must contend with, and master.

What I call *deep debt* is the harm institutionalized by the cornerstones of industrial era capitalism. It can be conceived of as debt owed to people, communities, society, the natural world, or future generations. Debt is simply shifted costs and borrowed benefits, from an economic point of view. If I have done economic harm to you by borrowing a benefit of $10 *from* you—or shifting a cost of $10 *to* you—I am in your debt. Though industrial era capitalism's debt is often invisible and uncounted, it must be settled and repaid for prosperity to expand. If I don't repay you $10, no prosperity has been gained; we have simply moved the $10 bill from one side of the table to the other. Scale that up, accelerate it, and you get the precarious house of cards that is the modern global economy.

That's why, while capitalism is unquestionably responsible for prosperity, industrial age capitalism is *also* inextricably linked to crisis: it is the rule, not the exception. As Michael Bordo, director of the Center for Monetary and

Financial History at Rutgers University, puts it, today's macroeconomy "seems much more crisis-prone."[12] At the turn of the twentieth century, the probability of financial crash was 5 percent; at the turn of the twenty-first, it had more than doubled, reaching 13 percent. According to Lehman Brothers, the eighteenth century saw eleven crashes; the nineteenth century, eighteen; and the twentieth, thirty-three. Irony of ironies, the twenty-first century opened with a crash explosive enough to topple Lehman itself. Cost shifting and benefit borrowing are becoming a more and more frenzied game of economic musical chairs—yet, when the music stops, there's a bill to pay. The cornerstones of industrial era capitalism institutionalize economic harm, whose growing debt fuels recurrent, accelerating crisis.

Think of it as the crisis *behind* today's many crises. When you pause to reflect on it, whether the crisis in question is financial, like that of the noughties; environmental, like Deepwater Horizon's oil spill; or simply personal, like an obesity epidemic—all are underpinned *first* by a great imbalance that undercounts costs and overcounts benefits. Celebrated MIT thinker Peter Senge, coauthor of the groundbreaking *The Necessary Revolution,* puts it this way, "More and more people are beginning to sense that the mounting sustainability crises are interconnected—symptoms of a larger global system that is out of balance."[13]

The great imbalance isn't just a passing crisis of superficial financial debt, but a longer, slower, broader crisis of authentic economic debt: deep debt. The real debt crisis isn't what America owes to China, or what Europe owes to

Germany. It's the deep, ever-mounting, unpaid debt of harm that business as usual owes people, communities, society, the natural world, and future generations, whether denominated in oil spills, banking meltdowns, or carbon emissions. Today, countries, companies, and people are struggling to repay the deep debt incurred by yesterday's harm. The result is the slow, steady diminishment of prosperity.

Here's a slightly more technical way to think about it. Capitalism is founded on the equation of creative destruction. The cornerstones of capitalism as we know it systematically and chronically undercount the costs of destruction and overcount the benefits of creation. Undercounting destruction and overcounting creation lead to overdestruction and undercreation. When the costs of destruction are undercounted—as they were by risk measures and models at banks—the result is an *oversupply* of "bads": destructive products, like toxic loans. Conversely, when the benefits of creation are overcounted—as they were by food industry standards, like "aftertaste" and "mouthfeel," that marginalized authentic nutritional value—the result is an *undersupply* of "goods": products that result in authentic benefits, like healthful foods. In the great imbalance, industrial era capitalism's cornerstones institutionalize what economists call negative externalities—or negative impacts excluded from market prices—making them systematic, and on the flipside, deinstitutionalize or limit positive externalities—benefits not included in market prices. Its institutions produce *too much economic destruction for too little creation.* That's what the great imbalance means.

As distinguished scholars Danny Quah, Mary Kaldor, and David Held—all codirectors of LSE's Global Governance research center—have argued in the *Global Policy Journal,* twenty-first-century institutions must "invest directly in the provision of global public goods and the mitigation of global public bads."[14] Columbia University economist Jeffrey Sachs argues that next-generation institutions demand "not just cooperation that keeps global public bads at bay (until they reach crisis proportions) but cooperation that centers on creating global public goods."[15] The globe-spanning great imbalance—an oversupply of "bads" or overdestruction, and an undersupply of "goods" or undercreation—suggests that cost shifting and benefit borrowing are literally *institutionalized,* built into the cornerstones of industrial era capitalism. The sum of overdestruction and undercreation is the deep debt a society incurs. When its scale and depth are revealed, the result is inevitably, as Sachs suggests, crisis.

Step back into my allegory for a moment. Prosperity on an ark differs radically from prosperity in a game reserve. In our metaphor of yesterday's capitalism as a game reserve, economic institutions were built to organize daily hunting most efficiently. They matched the swiftest, most powerful hunters to the biggest game to generate prosperity. But if the rules of hunting are used to manage an ark, the result will be repeated crisis and eventual collapse. In big, empty, stable worlds, hunters can borrow benefits and shift costs with abandon, accumulating deep debt. Throw your bones away here. It doesn't matter. If you kill off this kind of fish, well, there's another in the next pond. Need cash? Capture some loot from the next tribe. It's not like you trade with them anyway. But in a tiny, crowded, fragile ark, everything counts. There's no one left to borrow benefits from or shift costs to: the destinies of all are inextricably interdependent. Prosperity—or its nemesis, crisis—accrues to everyone.

To gain an intuitive feel for twenty-first-century economics, put yourself at the helm of such an ark. You're the captain, and on board, every resource you've got isn't just valuable, but *in*valuable. Whether people, trees, animals, ideas, trust, creativity, or governance itself, you must safeguard all against damage, depletion, and exhaustion. Conversely, every resource you *do* decide to utilize must result in more tangible, meaningful, enduring benefits than merely ephemeral "product" to be overconsumed. Prosperity on an ark depends *first* on minimizing economic harm, because every cost you shift and benefit you borrow result in permanent, perhaps irreplaceable loss, with unpredictable chains of consequences. If you get the balance of authentically good "goods" and "bads" wrong, the result won't be prosperity, but deepening crisis and, perhaps, eventual collapse.

Here, then, is the predicament the global economy is in today. We're using rules built for hunting to manage an ark, but that approach to prosperity is past its sell-by date. The real crisis is bigger than banks, bonuses, or bailouts: it's that twentieth-century institutions aren't fit for twenty-first-century economics. They are a poor match for a tiny, crowded, and fragile world. The world has changed radically, but capitalism hasn't.

The Capitalists' Dilemma

Capital*ists* haven't changed either. The truth is that most companies see themselves more as hunters ("you eat what you kill," "business is war") than as . . . See? So unequipped are we for twenty-first-century prosperity, we don't yet have a word for the role analogous to "ark manager." Most of us are still firmly ensconced in the industrial age. We pay lip service to "sustainability"; some of us "empower" our employees; a few strive to be better "citizens," but for most of us, the daily rituals of capitalism remain much the same. What really matter, at the end of the day, are profit, growth, and shareholder value. And therein lies the first hint of a dilemma worthy of the great tragedian Euripides: built atop a great imbalance, *more* of the above fuel *less*, and *less meaningful*, prosperity.

After distilling the five cornerstones of industrial era capitalism, step two in our research was to build a statistical population of over two hundred fifty companies to sample. We included a multitude of different kinds of companies, for completeness: the largest publicly listed firms by market capitalization in both developed and emerging markets, the portfolio companies of top-tier venture capital and private equity funds, and noteworthy public and private companies that surfaced repeatedly in discussions with CEOs and analysts. Each was categorized and analyzed in terms of cornerstones. What was common to 90 percent of the companies was yesterday's set of cornerstones.

I'd like to suggest that industrial age cornerstones limit organizations to creating "thin" value. Thin value is the invisible *fist* of the great imbalance, the real-world expression of overproducing bads and underproducing goods. It has three defining characteristics and three iconic products of the past few decades—McMansions, Hummers, and Big Macs express it precisely.

- Thin value is *artificial*, often gained through harm to or at the expense of people, communities, or society. A McMansion for everyone was the rallying cry of the American economy in the nineties. Yet McMansions turned out to be a visceral example of artificial value, so worthless just a few short years later that many were abandoned and, in some cases, knocked down for lack of demand. Rather than financing broader home ownership, the complex, thinly documented loans that banks in the noughties originated, packaged, and traded yielded profits at everyone else's expense; first, at the expense of borrowers; then customers, like other banks; and ultimately, at the expense of society, through massive bailouts. Most businesses are like banks, just writ smaller. Rather than creating authentic economic value, they are simply transferring it from one party to another. One gains, and the other loses.

- Thin value is *unsustainable*, often "created" today simply at the expense of forgone benefits tomorrow. What is it, exactly, that drives so many people nuts about Hummers? That they are deeply unsustainable on almost *every* level, because they pollute many kinds of shared resources inordinately. They clog up not just the atmosphere, but also roads, neighborhoods, and, because they are heavily financed, financial markets. Most businesses are still the economic equivalent of Hummers: giant internal combustion engines that merely sacrifice tomorrow to enjoy today. Yet, just as the Hummer's profits were unsustainable—boosting GM's margins for less than half-a-decade—so thin value of every kind isn't built to last.

- Thin value is *meaningless,* because it often fails to make people, communities, and society durably better off in the ways that matter to them most. Do you benefit when you eat a Big Mac? It might taste great, but it has a tangible, negative impact on your health when consumed regularly. Who benefits when we all eat Big Macs? No one. Today, an obesity epidemic is gripping America and spreading across the developed world. Most businesses are still serving up the economic equivalent of fast food: negative-impact goods and services that fail to make people, communities, and society tangibly better off.

Thin value is, in these three crucial ways, not *authentic economic value* at all. Here's a hypothetical example of thin-value creation. Let's imagine you sell a widget that costs $8 to a customer for $10, realizing a profit of $2. How thin is the $2 of value you have created? Is it counterbalanced by losses to others, like society and communities? If those losses are more than $2, you have failed to create any *authentic* value.

Is it a gain realized by depleting more than $2 of the future value of a nonrenewable pool of resources? If it was, you failed to create *sustainable* value. Do customers actually realize the value they have paid for, in terms of durable outcomes? Your customer valued your good at $10. If he realized less than $10 net in terms of tangible, positive outcomes, you failed to create *meaningful* value. If any or all of the three conditions are met, congratulations, you failed to create authentic economic value. Just threadbare, thin value.

Today's great challenge is not merely in creating book value, business value, or shareholder value, but in creating authentic economic value. Let's go back to our burger. A burger yields roughly a dollar of profit, and under the rules of industrial era capitalism, a dollar of value, at minimum, is said to have been created. But the full cost of a burger is perhaps closer to $30, not $3. The dollar of value that has been created is an economic fiction: it's thin, inauthentic value. All that has happened is that burger makers have borne $2 of the burger's full costs and earned another dollar of artificial "profit." But up to $27 of economic harm is still done to people, society, and future generations. No authentic value has been created; the profit booked an illusion of imbalanced accounting. In fact, to create a dollar of *real* value, a burger would have to yield a dollar of profit not from a cost basis of $3, but from a cost basis of up to $30. That's a difference of *ten times*. Thin value's challenge is mega-scale, measured not just in a few measly percentage points, but in orders of magnitude.

Here's another way to think about thin value. A firm can be said to have created value when its returns exceed its cost of capital. Thin value is a set of returns that exceed only the financial cost of capital—the returns to debt and equity holders. The financial cost of capital falls economically short of the *full-spectrum cost of capital.* The full-spectrum cost of capital exceeds the cost of financial capital because it factors in the many different kinds of capital utilized in production—natural capital, social capital, and human capital, to name just a few. It factors in returns to holders of equity, financial debt, and deep debt.

The full-spectrum cost of capital is a higher standard. No company has yet mastered the art of measuring, applying, and monitoring it. But this much is certain: applying the full-spectrum cost of capital would instantly and radically devalue the profits of industrial era businesses, pushing many into de facto losses. How profitable would fast-food makers be if they had to bear the partial costs of obesity, carbon emissions, and malnutrition? That's thin value: profit that is in many ways a financial fiction, because it fails to exceed a fuller, truer economic cost of capital.

Bubbles and crashes come and go. Yesterday, dot-coms; today, mortgage derivatives. Yet, a broader economic crisis precedes and envelops transient bubbles and crashes—a crisis of authentic economic value creation. When profit is realized by activities that harm people, communities, society, the natural world, and future generations, the result is value of low quality, counterbalanced by deep, hidden debt. It is that trap that the bulk of companies can't escape.

The great dilemma of industrial age capitalism is that to create value for some requires borrowing benefits from or shifting costs to all others; that less prosperity is fueled by harsher crisis; that *less* creation demands *more* destruction. All three are faces of the same beast—yesterday's paradigm jarring discordantly against an interdependent world.

Caught fast on its horns, more and more of yesterday's giants—from Detroit automakers to Wall Street, the Gap, Sony, and Microsoft, to name just a few—are stumbling, tumbling, and falling. Why? Thin value is a mirage, what the economist Jack Hirshleifer famously referred to as "socially useless."[16] Ultimately, the failure to create authentic economic value catches up with every company, country, and economy. Thin value can be defended, hidden, force-fed, or fought for. But never for forever and rarely for more than a handful of years. The 90 percent of companies that can create only thin value are uncompetitive in twenty-first-century terms, for two reasons.

First, the hidden interest that must be paid on harm's debt is ever compounding. Because of, for example, lobbying requirements, raw materials prices, energy prices, low employee engagement, regulatory scrutiny, and more active resistance from people and communities, costs are continually intensifying for industrial age businesses. In the real world, for burger makers, interest is mounting on harm's debt. So, for all these reasons, burger making is less and less profitable.

Second, the debt of economic harm can be "called" by creditors at any time. Think of it as what trader and

New York University mathematician Nassim Nicholas Taleb has called a "black swan" event: an unexpected, unpredictable—yet unavoidable—catastrophe. Sooner or later, customers revolt, regulators act, investors flee, or worst of all, a competitor that *can* create authentic economic value and do less harm surfaces. If the debt of harm was called for burger makers—if burger makers had to bear the full costs of burger making because, for example, subsidies were yanked, and carbon and junk food taxed—what would be the result? Each burger would yield not a profit of $1, but a potential loss of $27. They would be instantly, irrevocably, irreversibly unprofitable, not just by a percentage point or two, but by hundreds or thousands of percent. Insta-collapse.

That's the scale of the challenge, the height of the hurdle, the depth of the dilemma that confronts countries, companies, and investors in the twenty-first century. Most can't even come close to answering it. And just as no fiercer hunter, sharper spear, or better coat of camouflage can help the inhabitants of an ark prosper, so no amount of orthodox strategy, innovation, or competition—all premised on economic harm—can help businesses, countries, economies, or the world reignite prosperity in the twenty-first century.

The Cornerstones of Twenty-First-Century Capitalism

So could the practice of capitalism, the art of *being* a capitalist, transform as radically over the next few decades, as it did during Adam Smith's era? I believe it can change, and

I believe more vitally that all of us *will* change it. Because the industrial age's great dilemma is like a Gordian knot—a problem that's simply unsolvable, vexingly intractable if we're still confined to thinking in yesterday's terms. The knot cannot be untied, but only *cut*. Escaping the capitalists' dilemma *requires* a paradigm shift.

To return to my allegory, the capitalism that fits an ark must do better than just managing today's hunting. It must match the economy's most productive soil and most threatened trees, animals, and plants with the best farmers and shepherds, so what was once scarce can grow abundantly. Twenty-first-century capitalism must organize the better saving and accumulation of every kind of productive resource for tomorrow. Its precepts and commandments must begin with minimizing economic harm and end with maximizing the creation of authentic economic value.

If we were to craft the crude, bare outlines of an updated economic paradigm—one that might have the power to blaze past yesterday's firewall of prosperity—what would be different about it, first and foremost, would be *optimization*. Here then are rudimentary sketches of the two fundamental *axioms* of such a paradigm.

The first axiom is about minimization: through the act of exchange, *an organization cannot,* by action or inaction, *allow* people, communities, society, the natural world, or future generations to come to *economic harm*. Both cost shifting and benefit borrowing are, remember, economic harm, which leverage up a company, country, or economy with deep, risky, costly, burdensome debt.

Conversely, the second axiom is about maximization: the fundamental challenge facing countries, companies, and economies in the twenty-first century is creating more value of higher *quality*, not just low-quality value in greater *quantity*. Think of it as *reconceiving value creation:* not merely creating larger amounts of thin, inconsequential value, but learning to create value of greater *worth*.

The great question that twenty-first-century economics asks is: must profit always require economic harm? A handful of revolutionaries today are answering no. Their answer, echoing across the global economy from Mumbai to Mountain View, Bentonville to Bangladesh, is a better kind of capitalism built for a tiny, fragile, and crowded world: constructive capitalism.

From our statistical sample of two hundred fifty companies, we found fifteen that were throwing yesterday's cornerstones out of the proverbial window. Our first surprise was who the constructive capitalists were: a motley crew, but not a ragtag one. They were some of the world's biggest companies and some of the smallest; some of the world's oldest companies and some of the newest; those that fit the stereotype of the forever nimble, radical innovator and those with reputations as lumbering giants. They cut across traditional industry, market, and geographic boundaries. We expected many more stereotypically game-changing start-ups to be insurgents, but we found that most were radical in name only. In contrast, many were companies we *least* expected to be discontented with industrial era capitalism's status quo, like Walmart, Nike, and Unilever (see table 1-1).

TABLE 1-1

Insurgents and incumbents

Insurgents	Incumbents
Apple	Sony
Google	Yahoo!
Tata	General Motors
Nintendo	Sega
Threadless	The Gap
Lego	Mattel
Interface	Dixie, Mohawk
Unilever	Kraft
Nike	Adidas
Whole Foods	Safeway
Walmart	Target
Banco Compartamos	Citigroup
Starbucks	McDonald's
Wikimedia	Britannica
Grameen	Vodafone, HSBC

You might notice that the last two organizations on the insurgents' list in the table aren't orthodox businesses. Grameen is a family of social businesses, and Wikimedia can be loosely classified as a nonprofit. Yet, both have created significant, industry-changing amounts of value, and by doing so, they have unleashed disruption on orthodox capitalists across industries, forcing them to alter their competitive decisions drastically. That's why we included them.

Constructive capitalists aren't just building better products, services, strategies, or business models: they are building better institutions *first*. It isn't a capitalism that J. P. Morgan or John D. Rockefeller would recognize, unless

they looked at the income statements of constructive capitalists. It is composed of a disruptive new set of cornerstones, geared for the new economics of interdependence.

To delve into them, we compared the fifteen "insurgents" to a carefully chosen set of foils, the "incumbents" on the list in the table. These foils were peers—often fierce, historic rivals—of revolutionaries. The difference? They were *only* employing yesterday's cornerstones. This set of peers was a control group that we hoped would bring the differences between old and new cornerstones into stark relief. Since this was the real world and not a petri dish, we couldn't control for every difference, but we tried to match them as closely as possible in terms of size, scale, scope, and intent.

After exhaustively studying both sets of companies through case studies, financial modeling, and interviews, we synthesized our data. Not only were the insurgents utilizing new cornerstones, a *common* set seemed to be emerging. Of the roughly fifteen companies that were revolutionaries, each was using one, two, three, or more of a shared set of new cornerstones. These cornerstones contrasted starkly with their twentieth-century equivalents. The insurgents weren't just disrupting the status quo; they were building something new in its place—new foundations for twenty-first-century capitalism. We came to call them constructive capitalists—and what they were building, constructive capitalism. Its cornerstones are shown in table 1-2.

What made the constructive capitalists different? I'll spend the next several chapters taking you on a guided tour of each new institutional cornerstone—and then discuss

TABLE 1-2

Industrial era capitalism's cornerstones vs. constructive capitalism's cornerstones

	Industrial era capitalism's cornerstones	Constructive capitalism's cornerstones
How production, consumption, and exchange happen	Value chains	Value cycles
Which products and services are produced, consumed, and exchanged	Value propositions	Value conversations
Why production, consumption, and exchange happen	Strategies	Philosophies
Where and when production, consumption, and exchange happen	Protection	Completion
What is produced, consumed, and exchanged	Goods	Betters

how you can begin building each. For now, here's a quick explanation:

- To utilize resources by renewing them instead of by exploiting them, the constructive capitalists were shifting from *value chains* to *value cycles*.

- To allocate resources democratically and respond better to demand and supply shocks, they were shifting from *value propositions* to *value conversations*.

- To become more competitive over the long term instead of just blocking competition temporarily, they were shifting from *strategies* to *philosophies*.

- To create new arenas of competition, instead of just dominating existing ones, they were shifting from *protection* to *completion* of their marketplaces.

- To seek meaningful payoffs that mattered in human terms, not just financial ones, they were shifting production and consumption from *goods* to *betters*.

No insurgent is carving every new cornerstone—yet. In fact, every single insurgent on our list is still utilizing at least one *old* cornerstone, and most are still utilizing several. What makes them insurgents, in contrast, is that they are carving, with intensity and commitment, at least one *new* cornerstone. That is how they differ from their industrial era rivals, whom are still utilizing *all* the old cornerstones.

Today's revolutionaries are *institutional innovators:* they're reconceiving not just products, services, or business models, but the foundations that products, services, and business models are grounded upon in the first place. The new cornerstones that constructive capitalists are carving operate at a more fundamental level: they order and organize production, consumption, and exchange. Listen to how John Hagel III, guru of corporate strategy and cochairman of the Deloitte Center for Edge Innovation, one of institutional innovation's cutting-edge pioneers defines it: "[It] redefines roles and relationships across independent entities to accelerate and amplify learning and reduce risks." That's why, in the twenty-first century, "institutional innovation will trump either product or process innovation in terms of potential for value creation."[17] You can think of it as the cousin of what Gary Hamel, London Business School scholar and *The Future of Management* author, has termed management innovation. Institutions are sets of practices so familiar to us that they become literally institutional*ized,* frozen in place, like microchips of production, consumption, and exchange hardwired together.

The problem is, yesterday's economic silicon is as obsolete as a mainframe. Consider what Hamel has to say about the lack of higher-order innovation: "The practice of management seems to have evolved at a snail's pace. While a suddenly-resurrected 1960s-era CEO would undoubtedly be amazed by the flexibility of today's real-time supply chains... he or she would find a great many of today's management rituals little changed from those that governed corporate life a generation or two ago."[18] Replace *management* with *institutions* in those sentences, and you begin to get the picture.

But today's radical innovators are rapidly making up for lost time. As Peter Senge argues, over the last decade, a growing number of revolutionary organizations "have all, in their own ways, learned how to see the larger systems in which they live and work. They look beyond events and superficial fixes to see deeper structures and forces at play."[19] And innovating those "deeper structures"—institutions—is, today, a better bet than churning out new products, services, strategies, or business models; it's what is truly scarce, rare, and hard to imitate.

The shares of publicly traded constructive capitalists outperformed market indexes such as the S&P 500, the NASDAQ, and the Dow Jones Industrial Average—not just

incrementally, but by leaps and bounds. Imagine yourself, for a moment, in the finely crafted brogues of a harried fund manager. If you place your money in a capacious enough basket of equities—over the medium term, at least—you can't lose: right? Wrong. In stark contradiction to the conventional wisdom, in the noughties, equity was a strikingly poor bet. Markets suffered one of their worst periods ever, bar none—a decade of flatlining that ended in spectacular value destruction. If you had invested $1 million in the S&P 500 at the turn of the twenty-first century, you would actually have *lost* money a decade later: you would have only about $800,000 left (that is, if you still had your job). But while the equity markets stagnated, the stock prices of constructive capitalists held ground, gained ground—and sometimes, skyrocketed. So if you had instead invested $1 million in the constructive capitalist portfolio, you would have become $3 million richer, more than tripling the money under your care (and probably earning a few satisfying bonuses along the way). That's the power of twenty-first-century economics at work: during the most stagnant decade in financial history, a difference in returns of over 300 percent.

Yet, truth be told, the market is a weak null hypothesis to test against. A measure of lowest common denominator, it yields inconclusive results that are overly sensitive to an anonymous, unreliable, overaveraged baseline. And shareholder value isn't a reliable measure of whether authentic economic value has been created. It is value that can be transferred from other stakeholders, rather than created anew.

So my team dug deeper. That dramatic ability to create shareholder value reflected that, in nearly every case—as for Apple, Nintendo, Google, Nike, and Lego—constructive capitalists tended to lead their industries, not just in terms of shareholder value, but also, often, in profitability and growth. Meanwhile, the profitability and growth of our control group of peers—their nearest rivals—tended to decay, often terminally.

But finding *that* is a far cry from explaining *what*. Just catching a glimpse of a relationship doesn't explain what, if anything, drives it. Hence, I don't claim that simply laying down a new cornerstone—or failing to do so—will, without fail, determine every last morsel of a company's near-term profitability. Rather, mere financial performance always reflects a deeper competitive context, and peeling back the layers of that onion reveals the core of the story. What's the missing link between cornerstones and performance, institutions and returns? In a word, *advantage*.

I want to trace the arc of a bigger story of an economic quantum leap—a voyage beyond the known universe of industrial age economics. Insurgents had the power to attain *next-generation* efficiency, productivity, effectiveness, and agility, while incumbents could only attain what their industrial era precursors had. Like superweapons pitted against switchblades, the less powerful latter are no match for the supercharged former.

Apple didn't just incrementally outperform Sony. Its vault past mere technical productivity to *socio-productivity* left Sony reeling. Google's jump to the outer limits of

evolvability let it craft, hone, and refine services at a pace so furious that Yahoo! was rendered irrelevant and, like Sony, facing an increasingly uncertain future. Walmart's ascension from mere operational efficiency to *socio-efficiency* continues to raise it head and shoulders above Target. Nike's leap from operating effectiveness to *socio-effectiveness* is obliterating Adidas and Puma. All echoed strikingly what Lego is doing to Mattel, Nintendo did to Sega, Tata is doing to GM, and what Threadless is in the nascent stages of doing to the Gap. Let me caution here that it's not that the companies on the list of insurgents are in some way *perfect*, unblemished, or impeccable. It's that they're *better*, economically.

The unexplored cosmos at that quantum leap's end? Constructive capitalists are able to turn thin value on its head and create *thick* value instead—*value that matters, value that lasts, and value that multiplies.* Think of thick value as value that's meaningful in human terms, reflecting durable, tangible gains, which aren't counterbalanced by the two kinds of economic harm. Insurgents create thick value when they generate profits by activities whose benefits accrue sustainably, authentically, and meaningfully to people, communities, society, the natural world, and future generations. To illustrate, let's go back to burgers: a burger that created thick value would either minimize, over the long run, *all* its $30 of full-spectrum costs to less than $3 or, conversely, be so irresistibly well crafted that it was able to command a price greater than $30. Never easily, always imperfectly, rarely completely, each insurgent is learning to bridge those gaps, in its own unique way.

Yet protecting people, communities, society, the natural world, and future generations from economic harm is exactly what most companies *can't* do. The ability to create thicker value than rivals by outperforming in terms of next-generation economics is, I'd like to suggest, the next level of advantage: a *constructive advantage.* Here's what the new cornerstones that insurgents are using can do that yesterday's cornerstones can't: rebalance the scales of the great imbalance. Insurgents could minimize harm and maximize authentic, sustainable, meaningful value, but incumbents couldn't. The result is constructive advantage. Each new source of constructive advantage is the consequence of real-world mastery of a new cornerstone, of learning to employ a new institution with power, poise, and precision.

Constructive advantage is an advantage in both the quantity *and* quality of profit. When a firm earns *more* profit than rivals, it can be said to have a competitive advantage. And 90 percent of companies, trapped in the industrial era, still seek a competitive advantage. The problem with adversarial, zero-sum competitive advantage is that just because you've captured a larger share of profit in your industry or sector doesn't mean that pool of profit *hasn't* been earned by shifting costs or borrowing benefits to begin with: it is little guarantee that the profit you've earned *doesn't* stem from economic harm. In fact, your profits may simply reflect thinner and thinner value that is even more artificial, unsustainable, and meaningless than ever. That's the story of Wall Street, Detroit, and Big Food writ large. Only when a firm earns more and *higher-quality* profit than rivals

TABLE 1-3

Sources of competitive advantage vs. sources of constructive advantage

Sources of competitive advantage	Sources of constructive advantage
Cost advantage stems from a *value chain* that exploits resources until they are depleted.	**Loss advantage** stems from a *value cycle* that renews resources and makes waste useful.
Brands are promises that convey the benefits of a one-sided *value proposition.*	**Responsiveness** is the result of fluid, ongoing, many-sided *value conversations.*
Dominance of a marketplace is the zero-sum result of blocking competition by acting *strategically.*	**Resilience**, an evolutionary edge, is achieved by competing with an enduring *philosophy.*
Captivity of customers, suppliers, or regulators happens when a firm *protects* a marketplace from entry by competitors.	**Creativity** happens when companies strive to *complete* marketplaces, creating new arenas of competition.
Differentiation happens through skin-deep (or even imaginary) differences in the features or attributes broadly similar goods offer.	**Difference** happens when companies seek meaningful payoffs that matter; when companies produce *betters*, they literally *make a difference.*

can it be said to have a constructive advantage. The new sources of constructive advantage, detailed in table 1-3, are the living expression of being able to create more, higher-quality value than rivals.

Constructive capitalists have an advantage in the *kind* of value they are able to create, not just its amount. Because higher quality value is less risky, less costly, more defensible, and more enduring, it is usually worth more to stakeholders of every kind: people, communities, society, future generations, employees, regulators, and investors alike. As we will explore, Walmart, Nike, Apple, and Google aren't just out-competing rivals by creating more value. By creating more, higher-quality value, they are leaping to the next level of advantage. Like a strategic superweapon, constructive advantage threatens their rivals—like Sony, Yahoo, the Gap, and Target—that survive by eking out smaller and smaller amounts of low-quality profit, with not just strategic decay, but with institutional obsolescence.

That's what I mean when I say today's revolutionaries are rebooting capitalism. Of course, they're not doing it alone. Customers, investors, governments, and suppliers are holding hands with them every step of the way, rewarding them more for creating higher-quality value. Regulators across the globe are turning a keener eye to harmful practices across industries. In America, multiple industries are being reformed at once—health care, energy, and finance, to name just a few. China is getting serious about the environment, having finally passed air-quality regulation in May 2010—and it's been debating introducing the national equivalent of triple-bottom-line accounting since the 1990s. Investors increasingly look beyond financial numbers to assess the quality of profit, not just its quantity. Social responsibility measures such as KLD Research & Analytics scores, ethical indexes such as the Fraser Consultancy's Ethical Reputation Index, and corporate governance scores such as Institutional Shareholder Services' Corporate Governance Quotient all play a more and more integral role in making cold, dispassionate investment decisions. Once powerless, tuned-out "consumers" have become knowledgeable, sophisticated *customers,* who

demand more from a business than mere lowest-common-denominator stuff. They're increasingly choosing to buy from companies that matter, and pay slightly more for the privilege. And if you cynically think those buying decisions are a luxury, confined to rich countries, and that you'll handily outrun this tectonic shift in demand by plowing into China, India, or Malaysia—think again: that's exactly where research suggests that people prefer thicker value the *most*.[20]

The rub? From all angles, companies are forced to internalize the economic harms they do and, even tougher, to offer more authentic, sustainable, meaningful benefits that matter more in human terms. Companies that can do so realize a constructive advantage. That also means that, conversely, yesterday's sources of competitive advantage are being devalued: they aren't sufficient for creating thick value. Skin-deep differentiation, transient market share, a saturation-bombed brand, another half-penny of cost advantage—all offer only more and more arduous paths to outperformance, if they offer it at all. They're a losing hand in a world where the deck is fast being restacked in favor of high-quality profit. Yesterday, Walmart's ruthless mastery of cost cutting led to a world-beating competitive advantage, but also resulted in tremendous economic harm to people, communities, society, the natural world, and future generations by shifting costs to and borrowing benefits from them. Today, it might surprise you to hear that a new Walmart is shifting from competitive to constructive advantage, through an intense focus on taking both kinds of economic harm out of its enormous, globe-spanning commercial engine. Walmart is learning that, as the world shifts from the economics of a game reserve to those of an ark, competitive advantage is just table stakes. It is constructive advantage that fuels twenty-first-century outperformance.

Constructive advantage can be thought of as how free a company is of deep debt to people, communities, society, the natural world, or future generations. Like any kind of overleverage, deep debt—with its interest accruing at ever steeper rates—is a significant risk. It can be called by the aforementioned at any time, whether through taxes, regulation, or defection to rivals with *less* deep debt. Conversely, when a company minimizes deep debt, the risks and costs of overleverage shrink, reducing its full-spectrum cost of capital and boosting returns. When a radical new Walmart strives to right yesterday's economic harm, it is taking the first halting steps on the path to minimizing deep debt. Here, then, is the sequence of steps then, that from an economic perspective, is the defining hallmark of a twenty-first-century business. *Less* deep debt equals *higher*-quality profit and a *more* constructive advantage.

Constructive advantage is the key to escaping the iron cage of the capitalists' dilemma. It says: "We don't need to do economic harm to profit; in fact, the *less* economic harm we do, the *more* we profit." The competitive effect? Rivals still trapped by the capitalists' dilemma, those who can only create value through economic harm, *must* start taking back the costs they've shifted and giving back the benefits they've

borrowed, if they wish to remain in the game. Checkmate: it's constructive capitalists' new competitive edge for the twenty-first century.

Summing Up

When, millenia hence, our progeny build the hall of fame of humanity's greatest creations, I have a hunch: that, in the dusty "Extremely Ancient Prehistory" annex—right next to democracy, the scientific method, and the microchip—capitalism will probably occupy its own spotlit exhibit. It might feature a holo-deck replaying the great failure of central planning that Friedrich Hayek presciently divined; a 4-d demonstration of an invisible hand lifting billions out of global poverty, just as Adam Smith foretold; or the grand, enigmatic equation behind the pulsing waves of entrepreneurship that Joseph Schumpeter so elegantly described.

Yet, if they could beam a message to us today, they might just remind of us of the fable of the Coyote—as in Wile E. The gizmos he ordered from Acme, Inc., might have worked. But what Coyote could never overcome was his *own* inherent self-limitations; his lack of imagination, his shortsightedness, his insatiable fixation on short-term gratification, and his remarkable *in*ability to learn from the last time he got blown up. Hence, poor old Wile E spent his beleaguered existence falling off cliffs, getting run over by trucks, and doing faceplants directly into brick walls.

Your challenge, our descendants might counsel us, is much the same—to reimagine your own role as a capitalist, and in so doing, to build a capitalism that improves on the inherent shortcomings of its industrial age predecessor, without sacrificing its gains. In a global economy already shaken to its core by a historic crisis, those shortcomings have rarely been more apparent. The twenty-first century capitalist's agenda, in a nutshell, is to rethink the "capital"—to build organizations that are less machines, and more living networks of the many different kinds of capital, whether natural, human, social, or creative. And, second, to rethink the "ism": how, when, and where the many different kinds of capital can be most productively seeded, nurtured, allocated, utilized—and renewed. What we need, then, is a new generation of renegades, laying deeper, stronger institutional cornerstones.

While we may not want to admit it, instinctively, we know: to fully prosper demands *more* than the capacity to achieve the former sort of plenitude—whose depths have been mightily plumbed. It demands, more genuinely, the ability *not* to incur the latter, piling up deep debt—and, in their place, the capacity to make the most of every last bit of untapped human potential. So here's the twenty-first-century capitalists' agenda, in a nutshell. To rethink the "capital"—to build organizations that are less machines, and more living networks of the many different kinds of capital, whether natural, human, social, or creative. And, second, to rethink the "ism": how, when, and where the many different kinds of capital can be most productively seeded, nurtured,

allocated, utilized—and renewed. Put both together, and the promise is for companies, countries, and economies to climb to a higher level of advantage, to scale a steeper apex of achievement.

Hence, a new generation of renegades, laying deeper, stronger, broader institutional cornerstones. They aren't profiting *in spite of* making people, communities, society, and future generations better off—but *by* doing so. As we will discover, that is the essence of authentic value creation—which, when it grows, is what promises to reboot prosperity. By design, by instinct, sometimes by accident, what these companies are building is a better kind of business. By doing so, they just might be putting business as usual out of business.

Following the trail they're blazing is a journey undertaken in six steps: mastering the five new sources of constructive advantage and the new cornerstone each rests upon, and then, finally, learning to wield them with maximum effect. Though it will be rich with examples and anecdotes, the story I'm going to tell you is about *cornerstones,* not companies. The latter are there only to illustrate and illuminate the crags and contours of the former. The names of companies to which next-level advantage flows will inevitably change, but only because tomorrow's institutional innovators will lay down even more unshakable cornerstones.

The future belongs to constructive capitalists. Here's how to become one.

Chapter Two

Step One: Loss Advantage

From Value Chains to Value Cycles

HE FIRST STEP in becoming a constructive capitalist is learning to attain a loss advantage. It happens by turning a linear value chain into a circular value cycle. Here's how a few revolutionaries have started to make the shift.

. . .

It was the Death Star of companies: ultra-lean, ultra-mean, and the size of a planet. By exploiting natural resources, squeezing suppliers, and crushing communities, Walmart grew to become the biggest company in the world—and public enemy number one for a generation of activists and

reformers. But today, it's rebuilding with three suspiciously *benevolent* goals: to use 100 percent renewable energy, to achieve zero waste, and to sell only products that benefit the environment. The goal is, as ever, to gain efficiency, only this time, it's a radically constructive form of twenty-first-century efficiency that is priority number one in the notoriously Spartan meeting rooms of Bentonville.

The old Walmart's goal was cost advantage—the most primitive and simplest form of industrial era advantage. Cost advantage is the living embodiment of operating efficiency: minimize your own costs relentlessly, and both the boardroom and the economy will be better off. Walmart built the world's biggest company by minimizing labor, marketing, and input costs.

But there's a problem with mere operating efficiency. Firms impose a broad range of unseen, unintended, and unwanted costs on others—environmental costs, human costs, social costs, to name just a few—but because these costs are often invisible, they remain uncounted and thus are not minimized. These costs are often described as negative externalities or spillovers, a concept pioneered by Cambridge economist Arthur Cecil Pigou and refined over the years by thinkers as diverse as: MIT's Peter Senge (who has applied them to organizations); sustainability thought leaders Paul Hawken and Amory and Hunter Lovins (who have noted their impact on the natural world); and Nobel Laureates Joe Stiglitz and Amartya Sen (who have looked at their macroeconomic repercussions).[1] What's common to all their deep thinking might be said to be this insight: when the full spectrum of costs incurred hasn't been minimized, one kind of value is simply traded for another. The costs you minimize with one hand might simply be given back with the other—like a factory polluting a river, cars smogging up the atmosphere, or food that results in ill health. If stuff is "free," it's underpriced—and so we can overuse it. That's how pursuing pure operating efficiency has led too often to exploitation and depleted resources.

Who, then, are these costs shifted onto? Orthodox business is used to considering rivals, like competitors, buyers, suppliers, and complementors and striving to outdo them in orthodox terms, like operating efficiency. The constructive capitalists we studied, however, considered five foundational categories of stakeholders whom I refer to throughout the course of this book: *people, communities, society, the natural world,* and *future generations.*

So negotiating power might have let Walmart achieve "everyday low prices"—the living expression of operating efficiency—but only at the expense of hidden, uncounted environmental costs. Without paying the costs of maintaining, sustaining, and renewing those resources, given Walmart's size and reach (if it was a country, it would be among the world's twenty-five largest economies), natural resources might end up threatened, putting communities and society on the offensive. Adam Werbach, CEO of Saatchi & Saatchi S, a global sustainability pioneer who worked closely with Walmart to kick-start its great shift, explained it to me this

way: "Walmart initially took on its sustainability initiative as a defensive move. After its explosive growth in the 1990s as one of the most respected companies in the world, it was unprepared for the attacks it sustained, particularly from the labor and environmental community. As soon as they rose to the top of the *Fortune* 500 list, society's expectations rose as well."[2]

Society's expectations: today, a radical new Walmart is discovering that operating efficiency isn't enough to sustain lasting economic advantage. Constructive capitalism's better definition of efficiency is *socio-efficiency*. It means minimizing *all* the costs that production incurs, whether they are the orthodox costs directly accounted for by industrial era business or less visible costs to society, communities, the environment, and people. That's a fuller, more economically valid kind of efficiency, not just a partial efficiency, where only some of the costs incurred by production are addressed.

Achieving superior efficiency in twenty-first-century terms—socio-efficiency—results not in cost advantage, but in *loss advantage:* the first of the new sources of advantage constructive capitalists realize. Walmart is using it to reconceive the deep economics of production and consumption. Loss advantage means an advantage in minimizing a business's own direct costs, while *also* minimizing the social, human, public, and environmental *losses* the business imposes on other economic actors. Where businesses seeking a cost advantage are often irresponsible, shifting, hiding, and pushing costs onto others, businesses seeking a loss advantage are radically—indeed, disruptively—responsible: they take responsibility for the full spectrum of the costs and losses production incurs.

Operating efficiency can be seen as a tiny subset of socio-efficiency. It is efficient only in the weakest, smallest sense: the minimization of only the direct costs firms are *forced* to pay today by law, by social pressure, or by competition. Players seeking loss advantage are turning that kind of weak efficiency on its head: they strive to minimize *all* the costs they can find, protecting and shielding themselves from future regulation and from stakeholder and social pressure, and amplifying competitive pressure on rivals. In 2009, Congress passed the landmark American Clean Energy and Security Act, which sought to cap greenhouse gas emissions in the United States for the first time. Though it might not pass the Senate this year, here's the point. When, inevitably, a bill capping, limiting, or taxing carbon emissions does become legislation, players seeking a cost advantage will find their cost basis disrupted because they will have to pay carbon costs. Yet, if they had sought a loss advantage *yesterday,* they would have sidestepped this disruption, because, while rivals struggled, their carbon costs would have *already* been minimized, traded away, and offset.

A second kind of loss advantage happens when, by minimizing costs and others' losses, businesses are able to achieve *greater* cost savings than rivals only seeking a cost advantage. Consider the second of Walmart's new sustainability goals: to achieve zero waste. As it strives to minimize waste, losses to communities and society are minimized. Walmart

realizes greater cost savings than it did yesterday by having less waste to dispose of and incurring lower packaging and disposal costs.

That's just the beginning. Loss advantage-driven companies are often able to explode the tired industrial era distinction between high-priced goods that are good for you and low-priced goods that aren't. Minimizing consumers' costs makes what we offer them more valuable to them, while we also offer them low-cost goods in the first place.

Consider how Walmart's story differs from StarKist's. One day, StarKist executives decided responsibility was what people wanted, so they developed dolphin-friendly methods to catch tuna and charged a premium for it. Shock: consumers wouldn't pay extra for dolphin-friendly tuna.

StarKist's real challenge wasn't just creating a sustainable product and charging a premium for it: it was redesigning the whole business into one that could offer dolphin-friendly tuna *at an equivalent or lower price.* StarKist might have invested in sustainable fisheries or dolphin reserves (to "offset" and protect dolphin stocks) for example. Its goal should have been to minimize the social losses of foregone dolphins *while* minimizing its own costs.

But like too many businesses, StarKist just wanted to *shift* costs, not minimize them; unimaginatively seeking the same old thin value, StarKist saw society's losses as costs to be passed right back to people, instead of *minimized.* It wanted to, from an economic perspective, charge people a tax for the luxury of *not* having to put up with negative externalities.

That's so twentieth century, it hurts. Here's what twenty-first-century advantage looks like. Walmart (yes, Walmart!) has put nongovernmental organizations (NGOs) like the Marine Stewardship Council at the heart of its new supply networks. Together, Walmart and the council are working to bring to market exactly what StarKist didn't: sustainably harvested fish at a *lower* cost to consumers than unsustainably harvested fish.

StarKist's costs are likely to rise, because unsustainably harvested fish stocks are being rapidly depleted. Walmart's costs, in contrast, are likely to decline, as scale, learning effects, and greater abundance drive down the cost of sustainable fisheries harvesting. When those price curves cross, kiss StarKist goodbye.

That's a small aftershock of a larger earthquake taking place in Bentonville. The foundational source of advantage the new Walmart is seeking is no longer a cost advantage: it is a loss advantage. In so doing, Walmart is striving to reach a new level of efficiency by cutting its costs *and* society's losses, the first step in creating thick value.

So how does an organization shift past mere operating efficiency, achieve superior socio-efficiency, and gain a loss advantage? Loss advantage happens by reconceptualizing, reorganizing, and rebuilding production and consumption as a value cycle, instead of a value chain. Today's innovators are discovering that building cycles instead of chains is the key to renewing resources for tomorrow, instead of merely exploiting them today.

From Value Chains to Value Cycles

Twenty-first-century businesses are built on renewable resources that can be replenished at a faster rate than they are consumed. In an interdependent twenty-first century, renewable resources offer starkly better economics than nonrenewable resources. Renewable resources offer less risk of disruption at lower costs for replacement, maintenance, waste, and disposal. A diamond mine can create value for a few decades, but when it's depleted, the value dries up. So today, renewable resources have moved further up what Nobel Laureate Harry Markowitz termed the efficient frontier: usually, they can create more value, for less risk, over a longer time horizon.

It's the polar opposite of yesterday. Twentieth-century businesses were built on value chains—bigger, badder assembly lines, when you think about it—and value chains tend to lead firms to build *non*renewable resource bases. John D. Rockefeller transformed the American industrial landscape by vertically integrating the production, refinery, marketing, and distribution of oil into a globe-spanning value chain that defined an era, one that Standard Oil's management committee tightly controlled from a boardroom at 26 Broadway. Value chains are built for linear production, and, as in Standard Oil's value chain, linear thinking dominates. You can use it up, throw it away, and not worry about where it goes when it's gone, because that's someone else's problem.

the standard practise
of architecture : is linear production
"we are Exxon!" *our value*
chain is the same

Linear production is built to make stuff that "dies" after a fixed life cycle, over and over again. For example, Standard Oil's value chain drilled for, refined, piped, barreled, transported, marketed, and retailed oil. That's where the chain ended. To Standard and its offspring—Exxon, Mobil, Chevron, Unocal—oil "died" once engines had emitted it as carbon. Of course, at the end of the chain, waste doesn't die. It just gets passed on to society, communities, and people.

Twenty-first-century businesses are built on value cycles instead. In stark contrast to linear production, the essence of a cycle is circular production. Circular production adds a "back to life cycle" to the orthodox life cycle. Value cycles consider how resources are utilized after they're dead or no longer productive—how they are recycled, repurposed, and remanufactured into resources that are living or once again productive. They are built to not just to produce outputs but to *re*-produce outputs, from resources that can be renewed.

The goal of a value cycle is simple: waste nothing, replenish everything. Cycles utilize resources intensively *without* depleting them. In fact, at the limit, they yield a new kind of scale economy for the twenty-first century: *economies of cycle.* The more intensely, frequently, and durably that resources can be cycled, the more average costs drop, because each cycle amortizes and offsets the fixed costs of production, like plants, property, and people.

Value cycles add four novel segments to value chains to reconfigure them cyclically:

Remarketing—Which outputs should we reuse, cycle, and remanufacture? As I will explore, Interface accepts competitors' carpets and tiles as well as its own for recycling, reuse, and remanufacture.

Reproduction—What will we reuse, recycle, and/or remanufacture? Interface's radically innovative Cool Blue technology lets it reproduce new tiles from a variety of reusable and recyclable materials.

Reverse logistics—How will we reclaim discarded outputs to be reproduced? Interface's ReEntry service reclaims old carpets from anyone discarding them by partnering with social enterprises and charities that manage sorting, transportation, and sometimes donation.

Spinning—In which direction will value cycle? Value chains are one-way streets, but value cycles can spin in many different ways.

While the industrial era value chain looked like figure 2-1, the value cycle is shown in figure 2-2.

To understand how innovators are building value cycles, let's consider each new segment of the cycle in turn.

FIGURE 2-1

The value chain

Inbound logistics ⟶ Operations ⟶ Outbound logistics ⟶ Marketing ⟶ Service

FIGURE 2-2

The value cycle

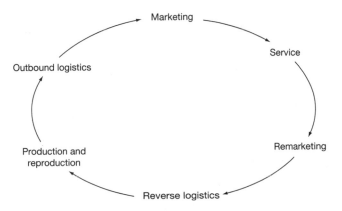

Radical innovators are shifting from value chains to value cycles: circular production networks designed for reclamation, reuse, recycling, and remanufacturing.

Remarketing

Remarketing has to do with understanding what kinds of resources are renewable and can be fed to a cycle and which aren't and can't be. To build a value cycle is to be able to feed it stuff that can be cycled. Conversely, only when a company understands what it is depleting can it understand what to renew instead.

Nike's Considered Index assesses the environmental footprint of its shoes. It measures waste through design and production, the toxicity of treatments such as harmful solvents, and the sustainability—in terms of energy use, water use, recycling intensity, and carbon impact—of the materials utilized in production. With the Considered

Index, Nike is beginning to understand how much its shoes deplete a broad range of natural resources—from the water table, to the atmosphere, to land utilized for landfills—and where to shift to renewable materials and inputs instead.

The Considered Index is the first plank of Nike's platform for corporate reinvention. Understanding what, where, and how Nike is depleting is the first step on a journey of deep, sweeping transformation. Using the Considered Index, Nike has pioneered a whole new approach to shoe design: Considered Design. It is built to "reduce waste throughout the design and development process, use environmentally preferred materials, and eliminate toxics."[3]

Considered Design is about designing high-performance shoes from the ground up, to never deplete and always replenish. It explodes yesterday's tired, industrial era dilemma in which performance, cost, and sustainability must always be traded off against one another. With Considered Design, Nike is able to produce shoes that are higher performance, more innovative, more sustainable, *and* better selling than its rivals' shoes. Today, Nike's best-selling running shoe, the Pegasus, is a Considered Design, reengineered from the ground up. It uses environmentally friendly, low-energy materials like water-based adhesives and recyclable rubbers and foams, such as Nike Grind, Nike's own recycled rubber, and cuts out unnecessary materials entirely. Result? A 13 percent lighter shoe with an 83 percent recyclable sole that commands better margins—better for runners, better for Nike, and better for society. Now *that's* thick value. It's no wonder that by

2011, Nike wants all its shoes to be Considered Design, all its apparel by 2015, and everything by 2020.

Nike is a master of remarketing. It is always asking, can we use reuse, recycle, repurpose, or remanufacture this input or output? If we can't, can we trade it to someone who finds it useful enough to compensate us for it? If we still can't, we have to find a way to strip it out of the cycle altogether, because cycles can't be fed with bad inputs that can't be recycled, reused, or repurposed. Considered Design is one of the world's most advanced ways of asking and answering these questions.

Reproduction

The Considered Index is just the beginning. Nike's goal for Considered Design is to shift to circular production, where, in the words of its vision, "anything and everything can be recycled into something just as desirable."[4] The Considered Index and Considered Design are the first and second steps. The third is that once Nike has discovered a mix of materials, processes, and treatments that isn't toxic, harmful, or wasteful, it can work on how to *reclaim shoes at the point of disposal.* Once it can reclaim shoes, it can *remanufacture* them at low cost, instead of producing completely new shoes—extending its newer, better kind of cost advantage.

A pioneer of value cycles, Nike's has been repurposing shoes since 1993. Two factories, one in the United States and another in Belgium, slice and grind shoes into rubber, foam, and fabric. The rubber is sold to create indoor soccer and

football fields, and the foam and fabric for basketball and tennis courts. Today, a twenty-first-century Nike hopes to push the boundaries of renewability further—from remarketing waste to reproducing products. Its goal is to be a company where every shoe bought is worn out and then brought back locally, perhaps to a Nike store, to be remanufactured into new Nike shoes, apparel, and sports equipment. Customers and society win, and so does Nike, whose margins promise to rise as cycle effects take hold.

Here's how Nike puts it: "Today, your worn-out athletic shoes can already live on in something new: a track, a basketball court, a playground. But tomorrow, our goal is that sports shoes, apparel and equipment will also be recycled into new Nike products. This way the materials we use will go through many cycles of design, manufacture and use. Just like bottles, cans and paper do now."[5]

Did you glimpse just how radical Nike's endgame is? It's a total rethink of how shoes are produced and consumed—one powered by renewal, not depletion. Where competitors see sustainability as a marketing exercise, Nike understands that a value cycle is the key to achieving a loss advantage and to building a next-generation business that competes by creating thicker and thicker value.

Interface, Inc., is taking the second segment in loss advantage even further by reproducing not only its own waste, but others. Meet CEO Ray Anderson, author of *Confessions of a Radical Industrialist*, who helped Walmart CEO Mike Duke craft and define his sustainability vision, and tutored Walmart's teams by showing them Interface's factories in action. Listen to his vision: "We want to drive the whole thing with sunlight, renewable energy, closing the loop on material flows so that you have not only the basic organic cycle we're all familiar with—the dust to dust cycle—but in an analogous way, a technical cycle that takes used-up products and gives them life-after-life through the recycling process, so that no molecules are lost."[6]

Not a single *molecule?* No wonder he told *Fast Company,* simply: "I want to pioneer the next industrial revolution" Interface's goal is to be the first flooring company that's "unhooked from the oil well."[7] Because vinyl and other petroleum by-products are key inputs to floors, accelerating oil scarcity is a time bomb for flooring companies. Interface already spins recyclable yarn from bio-based fibers made, essentially, from corn starch. But through ReEntry, its pioneering carpet reclamation and recycling program, Interface will reclaim rivals' carpets, as well as its own. Hence, ReEntry's slogan, "Interface wants your carpet"—and, in the near future, your old tiles, plastic bottles, and maybe even trash.

Yes, trash. Interface has developed a radical new manufacturing process for its Cool Blue carpet backing called Cool Blue, based at its plant in Lagrange, Georgia. Instead of using new raw materials for tiles and carpets, Cool Blue lets Interface remanufacture new carpets and tiles with old ones and lots of other stuff besides. Cool Blue can make tiles and carpets out of corn, instead of oil, and because corn is renewable where oil isn't, Interface stands to realize a long-run cost advantage.

Think of the economics at work. Once materials are in Interface's value cycle, they stay in it: they can be perpetually reused and recycled. Because its food is everyone else's waste, Interface can obtain raw materials at lower cost. And here's the kicker: as its already low-cost inputs are used over and over again by the cycle, their average costs drop to zero for both Interface *and* society—thicker and thicker value. As Anderson observes to AltEnergyStocks, "Over 15 years we've demonstrated that sustainability is a better way to a bigger and more legitimate profit."[8]

By doing good for everyone, Interface is doing good for itself. The more it utilizes Cool Blue, the more carpets and tiles Interface can make without using new oil and the better off people, society, the natural world, and Interface are.

Yet not everything can be so easily cycled. Like every other business, Interface still uses energy and emits carbon. Interface can't reclaim and recycle these alone. So to counterbalance those costs, it has shifted to sourcing green energy produced renewably from, for example, wind farms and geothermal plants. Carbon is offset by investing in carbon credits and in carbon-reduction projects. Interface bought emission-reduction credits from, for example, a wind farm in New Zealand. Though often criticized by environmentalists, offsetting is a way to circularize production by *outsourcing* the completion of an ecocycle to others, which renew our waste for us. Because offsetting is vulnerable to the same information problems and conflicts of interest (such as ensuring your subcontractors uphold your own high standards) that can surface in most outsourcing relationships, it's not always the most efficient way to complete a cycle. Yet, for many, it is an easy way to explore the new economics of circular production.

Many businesses are striving to be carbon-neutral. Yet, for Interface, that is just table stakes. It offsets carbon and buys green energy to achieve a neutral-waste position. But Cool Blue lets Interface become *waste positive* by reclaiming other people's waste, actually minimizing the total amount of waste in society. Or, from an economic point of view, minimizing everyone's losses, because waste is a net loss. That's authentic loss advantage: striving not just to be waste neutral but to be waste positive, replenishing *more* than you deplete.

Interface is perhaps the world's single most-renewable business today, built almost entirely on renewable resources. That's true twenty-first-century business, because Interface is no longer at the mercy of accelerating resource scarcity or the market mayhem that ensues.

Interface makes the radical sound easy. But orthodox capitalism still holds most businesses fast. Consider how radical the impact of cycling might be on an industry like fast fashion. There, the turnover in products—and the waste generated by consumers churning through disposable clothes on a weekly basis—is immense. Topshop can introduce as many as three hundred new designs in its London store every week. By accelerating the pace of production in fashion, Topshop (and its rivals Zara and H&M) have also ensured that unwanted clothes pile up faster. Though Topshop has responded to sustainability concerns by, for example, buying more Fair Trade cotton, in this industry, cycling is

inevitable, because the first player to remanufacture everyone *else's* clothes, like Interface recycles rivals' carpets, will realize a significant loss advantage. It will ultimately be able to produce new outputs more cheaply, quickly, and reliably than the same old industrial era value chain can produce them.

Cycling simply means discovering how intensively waste can become food. Scale economies create a powerful incentive to utilize resources at 100 percent capacity: to churn out as much stuff as possible to bring down average costs. In cycle economies, incentives change radically: average costs drop not in output, but in the number of times an input can be reused and recycled. For Interface and Nike, the average cost of carpets and shoes drops the more they can be remanufactured, as the same plastic, rubber, foam, and other raw materials cycle and recycle through a loop, from products to waste and back again. What is crucial is that they don't have to be bought and paid for anew each time.

Reverse Logistics

The third segment of a value cycle is reverse logistics, and the most efficient value cycles are the *shortest*. Value-cycle owners always have an incentive to move production as close to consumption as possible to minimize how far resources have to flow to be recycled, remanufactured, repurposed, and reused.

As Nike develops its value cycle, it will have to build out this new segment, ensuring that shoes don't just go from the factory to the athlete, but back from the athlete to the factory where they can be remanufactured. Interface has already built its recapturing team, ReEntry, that will pick up used Interface and competitors' rugs. Interface knows that the more free inputs to cycle and remanufacture, the lower average costs drop and thicker value can be created.

Spinning

The fourth segment in building a value cycle is spinning it. Who puts the cycle into motion? Value cycles can spin forward like orthodox, linear supply-driven value chains, where boardrooms pull the trigger that pushes goods through various stages of production. But they should spin backward. For the most value to be created, value cycles should be spun into action by demand, because letting customers pull resources ensures they are only utilized when called for, minimizing overstock, inventory, and finished-goods waste.

Walmart, Nike, and even Interface haven't built true value cycles yet. Their value cycles spin the wrong way, from supply to demand, rather than vice versa. So who has synced a value cycle the right way, letting demand spin up production?

Enter Lego, the unlikeliest of revolutionaries. Five years ago, Lego was on the brink of bankruptcy and in deep strategy decay. Today, it is earning record profits—growing its operating margin from 5 percent in 2005, to nearly 25 percent today—while rivals like Hasbro and Mattel are fighting for dear life—thanks in no small part to slashing yesterday's

businesses and investing in tomorrow's. At Lego Factory, I can upload my own design for a Lego set, which Lego will produce for me, bundling only those bricks I need. Demand spins up the value cycle, instead of boardrooms putting the gears of production into action.

Lego Factory doesn't recycle and renew bricks—yet. It recycles ideas. I can upload a design that *you* can reuse and build on. Instead of starting from scratch to design new Lego sets, we can alter each others. Lego realizes instant efficiency gains, dropping the cost of developing and designing new Lego sets. Lego always has a renewed stock of ideas for Lego sets to draw upon. So Lego Factory is a value cycle where *soft* resources like ideas and designs are reused to make the use of *hard* resources—bricks—more efficient, creating thick value.

Lego Factory doesn't just minimize Lego's costs. It minimizes customers' losses as well. The same bricks are turned into designs that match individual customer preferences more efficiently. Because I am getting exactly the Lego set I want, fewer resources are wasted. Customers don't have to order Lego sets they don't want, just for the sake of a few choice bricks, and Lego doesn't have to take the risk of producing sets that are no longer in demand. Like Nike's Considered Design, Lego Factory explodes an industrial era trade-off. It minimizes waste, effort, and duplication, *while* maximizing satisfaction and creativity. Lego is creating thick value in toys—achieving a loss advantage—through a value cycle that is spun by demand, which radically reconceives toy design and production.

To utilize a cycle to achieve a truer, fuller loss advantage—to maximize thick value—the cycle must renew all the capital that the firm is utilizing or affecting. No company has yet gone that far, but some of the companies discussed in this chapter might get closer.

Consider the Lego Factory, which cycles ideas, not bricks. But Lego could extend the Lego Factory into a broader value cycle where it can both recycle and reuse ideas *and* bricks, deepening its loss advantage. Customers might be able, for example, to design their own Lego sets and then recycle their old sets into the new ones by mailing old bricks back to Lego. Result? Even thicker value than Lego creates today.

Walmart is notorious for destroying social capital in the communities its stores serve. When it puts the local butcher, pharmacist, and baker out of business, it destroys focal points for local interaction. How could it renew that social capital? By making social capital part of the cycle. It could let its stores be reused as places for community activities, like civic meetings, elections, or day care. Or it could reuse local businesses themselves by giving local businesses a home inside Walmart stores, turning Main Street inside out. In turn, doing so could offer Walmart new customers, new revenue streams, better information, and more trusted, lasting relationships with people. Blue sky ideas? Ask yourself if, a decade ago, you would have thought that Walmart would be leading the charge for sustainability. Perhaps a decade from now, Walmart will be taking even more radical steps in the quest to consistently thicken value.

Summing Up

Yesterday, Walmart built the world's biggest business with small but steady gains in operating efficiency. Nike sought a cost advantage by simply outsourcing production to developing countries. Today, like Interface, both are realizing that twentieth-century efficiency cannot power twenty-first-century advantage. Today's challenge is achieving a better kind of efficiency altogether: socio-efficiency that minimizes both direct costs and full-spectrum losses, creating thicker value. To achieve gains to next-generation efficiency, all three—Walmart, Nike, and Interface—are innovating the cornerstone of industrial-age production itself: they are producing not in lines, but in circles. They are doing this not out of altruism, but because doing so unlocks radical new paths for strategy, competition, and ultimately a new source of advantage: loss advantage. Simply, renewing resources for tomorrow is wiser than exploiting them today.

Are you taking the first step to becoming a constructive capitalist? Here's a quick checklist.

Social/cultural
economic
environmental
Ven diagram

First, a value cycle must be fed with good inputs. Are you assessing the full-spectrum costs—environmental, social, and human—of the raw materials and inputs that you use? Do you have a tool like the Considered Index that assesses whether inputs are cyclable—whether they can be reused, repurposed, recycled, or remanufactured? Are you grappling with the more meaningful economic calculus of the twenty-first century?

- Second, inputs and outputs must travel around a cycle—with the least amount of loss possible. How high up the ladder of reusing, repurposing, recycling, or remanufacturing have you climbed? Have you turned an industry age assembly line circular? How intensively are your costs dropping as resources cycle?

- Third, the time and space between production, consumption, and reproduction should be shortened to further amplify cycle efficiency. Does your cycle still operate over vast, energy-sucking distances—how long is it? Does your cycle require inventory costs, carrying costs, and working capital—how sluggish is your cycle?

- Fourth, and most powerful, value cycles must be spun. Who spins the gears of production—or reproduction—into motion? Which way does your cycle spin—forward, from supply to demand, or backward, from demand to supply?

Step Two: Responsiveness

From Value Propositions to Value Conversations

O YOU'VE BUILT a value cycle and gained a loss advantage. The next step in becoming a constructive capitalist is mastering *responsiveness,* upping the speed, accuracy, and agility of a value cycle. Responsiveness happens by turning top-down, take-it-or-leave-it value propositions into deeply democratic value conversations. To see what that looks like in practice, let's take a closer look at one of our insurgents.

. . .

How many decisions does your boardroom make per minute? That's right. Not per year, quarter, month, or day. Per minute.

One company makes more—and better—decisions faster than any other. It just might be the world's smartest organization. By the time most companies have made a single decision, Threadless has made thousands, without even furrowing its brow, much less breaking a sweat.

It's a clothing start-up that's revolutionary in every way. Art students Jake Nickell and Jacob DeHart were so inspired by a simple T-shirt design competition that they invested $1,000 in seed money to start Threadless. Their big idea? *Anyone* can submit designs for T-shirts—and then, *anyone* can vote for the designs they like best. The ten highest-ranked designs are produced weekly, in limited editions, with a fee flowing back to designers. The result is a business that's more like a living, thriving marketplace—controlled directly by customers.

Now if you're thinking, "…but it's just a T-shirt company," think again. Here's why what Threadless is doing matters to you. That radical new approach to managing T-shirt production has yielded growth and profitability in an industry almost entirely bereft of it. Yesterday's giants—Gap, Tommy Hilfiger, and Nautica—have spent the last decade struggling with a long, slow, seemingly irreversible slide into decline. If you'd invested $1,000 in Gap a decade ago, you'd only have $700 left. But if you'd put $1,000 in Threadless—like Jake and Jacob—you'd have built a business worth, by my informal estimate, more than $100 million, growing by leaps and bounds, already enjoying industry-leading margins, slowly but surely wresting market power from them.

Threadless is the reigning global champion of the second source of constructive advantage: responsiveness. It is the most responsive company in the world, bar none, because responding to change has become an effortless reflex. If T-shirts with LOLcats are in fashion this month, Threadless can make them instantly. If T-shirts with ninjas are in fashion the next, Threadless can respond. T-shirts about wolves were hot in 2009 (no, really, just ask your local teenage hipster). Gap will make them after they're fashionable—maybe. But Threadless knows about them *before* they were in fashion. It helps propel the trend.

Like the lumbering clothing giants of yesteryear, most companies are ploddingly, ponderously unresponsive, because it takes a great deal of time and effort to make new decisions accurately. A great many can't make accurate decisions no matter *how* much time and how many resources or mega-consultants they've got. Consider Gap, Inc.—for whom a decade of strategy decay has resulted from a seeming inability to make timely, accurate decisions about, well, what clothes people really want. Result? Lukewarm designs that are lambasted by critics, shunned by once-loyal customers, and ignored by today's youth. Perhaps it's no surprise that Gap's share price has fallen by 50 percent over the last decade, reflecting stagnant growth.

Just as loss advantage stems from achieving greater next-generation *efficiency* than rivals, so responsiveness is built on a new economic foundation. It stems from achieving greater next-generation *agility* than rivals.

Orthodox capitalism was concerned with operating agility. Given the same factories, people, and raw materials, can we produce razors instead of toothpaste? Can we produce word processors instead of typewriters? Can we produce electric cars instead of gas guzzlers? A machine that would let us make any product in the world in the blink of an eye would make us maximally, operationally agile. Today, there are more than four thousand suppliers willing to strike a bargain with you at Shishi Clothing City, the largest garment market in China's Fujian Province. And that's just the tip of an iceberg: Hongxiu Clothing City, China Clothing City, and Huanan Market City are right in neighboring Guangdong. Any garment, anytime? We're talking about the epicenter of mere operating agility's commoditization.

Strategic agility is concerned with diversifying where, when, and to whom we can sell. A machine that would let us employ any business model in the world to sell our stuff in the blink of an eye would make us maximally, strategically agile. That's what Gap was trying to approximate when it created Banana Republic and Old Navy: new ways to market, distribute, and sell clothes. The Gap's ongoing problems point to the shortcoming of strategic agility. Rapid entry and exit from markets often indicate a lack of a sustainable, meaningful impact in any.

Managerial agility is agility updated for the twenty-first century. It isn't the ability to produce better products, services, business models, or strategies faster than rivals. It is the ability to produce better *decisions* faster than rivals. Given the same competitors, buyers, suppliers, and customers, can we decide that subscriptions are worth more than transactions in the first place? Can we decide that electric cars are more valuable than gas guzzlers? Can we decide that six-bladed razors are worth more than a fundamentally new approach to shaving? Can we decide that T-shirts about dogs are more valuable than T-shirts about cats? How rapidly, consistently, and accurately—if at all—can we do so?

It's brains over brawn, and Threadless has it in spades. Imagine a machine that would let us make any decision, in the blink of an eye. It would, if we could make any decision accurately, no matter how tough, complex, or risky, instantaneously make us maximally, managerially agile. Threadless comes strikingly close to achieving that in apparel. Threadless is able to make more accurate decisions about *what to produce* better than rivals, because always-on voting by consumers reveals preferences in real time. As those preferences are aggregated— as votes are counted and weighed—Threadless effortlessly knows what is optimal to produce. Through the participation of customers, the costs of managerial decision making are lowered to almost nil: no meetings, no managers, no memos. In contrast, the costs of making new decisions for nearly every company in the world are orders of magnitude higher than for Threadless.

"Better decisions faster." Say it fast ten times, because it is Threadless's secret. Gap, Tommy Hilfiger, and Nautica are busy imitating one another, and Shishi, Hongxiu, and Huanan clothing cities are in hot pursuit, imitating *them*. Next stop, discount rack. In a world where anyone can make, market, and retail 10 billion kinds of jeans, socks, and

are we the Gap?

T-shirts almost instantaneously, the question becomes: what is most worth producing in the first place? Rivals struggle, flounder, and imitate one another endlessly, because for them, that decision is costly, tough, and complex. But for Threadless, it's easy to consistently make choices they've never even imagined, that customers love.

Think thick value: Threadless churns out innovative new T-shirts day after day after day after day, while Gap struggles to eke out a dozen barely interesting ones per *season*. Responsiveness has exploded its capacity to innovate. At Threadless, newer, better decision making isn't something that happens in quarterly meetings. Instead, it never stops happening in the first place. As Jake Nickell explains, "The voting mechanism was used to figure out what would get made—we couldn't make everything so we might as well just make the best stuff!" The key word is *best*. Threadless wanted to find a more effective way to decide what the best, most innovative T-shirts were.

Though it might sound complicated and messy, Threadless is a well-oiled, finely honed machine. Through its always-on voting system, the fuss and muss of top-down decision making are largely eliminated: designers submit new T-shirt designs, customers click, Threadless counts up the votes, and spins the wheels of production into action.

When a company gets responsive, product, service, business model, and strategic innovation happens almost automatically. It takes years to perfect a golf swing. What if, after seeing Tiger Woods swing a nine iron once, the perfect swing was built into you reflexively, just like blinking?

That's the difference between innovation and responsiveness. Threadless isn't mega-innovative because it can make different styles of T-shirts, but because it can make new decisions *about* better T-shirts in the first place.

So how can you achieve managerial agility and gain responsiveness?

It's time to meet Threadless's cousins, siblings, and grandparents. Threadless, after all, is just the kid brother of a large, vibrant, extended family. Today, radically democratic businesses are rethinking *how* decisions are made from the grass roots up.

From Value Propositions to Value Conversations

How does responsiveness happen? Twentieth-century businesses were built for value propositions, but twenty-first-century businesses are built on a new institution: the value conversation. Twenty-first-century organizations don't manage by monologues solemnly intoned from the inside out and the top down. They manage through dialogue that starts from the outside in and the bottom up. By democratizing decision making in a multitude of ways, constructive capitalists are *able* to allocate resources with maximum agility.

how would this translate @ Rothhurst

Markets allocate resources through what's supposed to be a shareholder democracy, yet the shareholder democracy industrial age capitalism built is the weakest kind of democracy. It is indeed in many ways a mockery of authentic democracy. Every shareholder has a vote, but almost no shareholder has a voice. For example, shareholders in the United States can't nominate directors unless they own more than 2 percent of outstanding shares.

Feeble shareholder democracy quickly becomes iron-clad managerial autocracy. After markets come boardrooms, and there's little democracy there. If companies were countries, we'd say they had centrally planned, dictatorial economies. So perhaps it's no surprise that companies embody the same inertia, rigidity, and tendency to misallocate resources that plagued—and, ultimately, brought down—yesterday's centrally planned nations in a globalizing, opening world. As the authors of *Wikinomics* and *Blur* have pointed out, boardrooms that command and control are inherently unresponsive in a world where change happens faster than the managerial hand can move.[2] Why? Because in bureaucracies, matrix organizations, and other forms of industrial era organization, the costs of making any decision are steep. Think of management as we know it as the equivalent of an assembly line: each decision must be made in a linear way, up or down the chain of command.

Constructive capitalists embrace instead democratic decision making. Now, here's the catch. Authentic democracy is an unexplored country. Democracy isn't what takes place in capital markets, nor in boardrooms. Nor is it *just* about voting, and neither does it mean *every* decision an organization makes is subject to the tyranny of the mob, as thinkers as disparate as Plato, the Harvard political scientist Archon Fung, and economics Nobel Laureates Elinor Ostrom and

Kenneth Arrow have suggested. Rather, authentic democracy is *participative, deliberative, associative,* and *consensual.* Those are the four freedoms at the heart of value conversations. Twenty-first-century organizations are democratic because the freedom to participate, the freedom to deliberate, the freedom to associate with peers, and the freedom of dissent let managers, customers, communities—and even competitors—hold conversations about *what is valued* and *what thicker value is.*

Participation means that those affected most by managerial decisions have the right to take part in them. *Deliberation* means that participants can reason, not just vote, to reveal different perspectives and values. *Association* means public spaces for that deliberation to take place unencumbered. And *dissent* is the only path to a truly meaningful, authentic *consensus.* In combination, the four freedoms allow decision making to become radically more agile.

Participation

Who gets to participate in a firm's decision making? Under the terms of orthodox capitalism, it's shareholders and shareholders alone—because they hold equity. Yet equity is a word with two interlinked meanings: the right to *share in a stream of profits,* and the right to *participate in decisions that affect your outcomes.*

Constructive capitalism's radical innovators are deepening equity, so it hews to the latter meaning. They are discovering responsiveness happens better when boardrooms

give more parties than just shareholders the right to participate in decision-making—and doing so can be as simple as a vote.

At Threadless, anyone can log in, glance at a bunch of T-shirts, and vote with a click. My kid sister votes in less than ten seconds. As Jake Nickell puts it, "It would have been arrogant for us to just say we know what's best. The proper way to do this within a community where everyone respects each other is to find some sort of way for the community to come together to make decisions. Voting was an easy and effective way to do that."[3]

Of course, for most industrial age companies, empowering the community equals *dis*empowering layers of managers. Hence, responsiveness is more easily gained for start-ups, where there aren't layers of middle managers fighting to retain their empires. No surprise, then, that another radically responsive start-up, Jelli, promises to upend broadcasting. During the nineties and well into the noughties, radio stations became radioactive—irrelevant to listeners, of dwindling value to advertisers, and of questionable value to shareholders. Why? Numerous payola scandals in recent years have confirmed that what's mostly played on the radio isn't what listeners want to hear. It's what labels want to sell. That's what led to a value-destructive equilibrium for the entire industry, riven by bankruptcy, restructuring, and consolidation.

So what might happen if *you* could control what your favorite local station plays from your phone? That's what Jelli, a San Mateo, California, start-up, is counting on.

It was founded in 2009 by Mike Dougherty and Jateen Parekh, both start-up veterans (Parekh was Amazon's first Kindle recruit). In its own words, "Jelli is radio democracy, putting the airwaves in the hands of the listeners."[4]

Jelli is building a radically more constructive radio marketplace, where listeners, labels, and broadcasters *all* win. Radio stations sold out in the first place because figuring out what listeners actually wanted was *costlier* than simply taking record-label side payments. Jelli promises to revolutionize radio by democratizing decisions about what gets played. Already, stations from Boston to Syracuse to Philadelphia have signed on.

Think a track rocks, or think it sucks? There, via your Web browser, you or anyone else can vote in real time for what your local station plays. According to Dougherty, "Jelli empowers individuals and communities to control traditional broadcast programming in a real-time, continuous manner using the web."[5] A Jelli-powered radio station gains managerial agility: it is able to make better decisions faster. Like a giant scale, Jelli aggregates everyone's listening preferences, making it crystal clear what listeners really want to hear. The result is responsiveness: Jelli-powered stations can respond to changes in listener preferences effortlessly and rapidly.

For advertisers, the proposition is equally disruptive. Not only have Jelli listening numbers soared in markets where it was rolled out because Jelli gives people better music, but Jelli has better information about listening histories and preferences in local markets. It combines the informational granularity of the Web with the intimacy of local radio,

allowing advertisers to craft better ads and target them more carefully.

Jelli is a tiny start-up with a disruptive promise, and Threadless is a medium-sized business growing at warp speed. But here's a big business growing at a snail's pace that is redefining itself by getting participative. Walkers, a business within PepsiCo's Frito-Lay snacks group, produces potato chips. Recently, it decided to rethink how potato chip decisions are made. The potato chip market has become home to a damaging flavors war, where chip makers, to gain an edge with chip lovers, are spending ever more to develop new flavors with shorter and shorter half-lives. The first step: anyone could contribute new flavors of chips via Walkers's Web site. People submitted 1.2 million new ideas for flavors. The second step: Walkers chose six of the most promising flavors to produce and distribute in small test batches. People tasted the new flavors. The third step: everyone voted on the flavor they liked best, that they wanted to be mass produced.

Some of the six new flavors chosen were those a boardroom would never have cooked up—like Fish 'n' Chips, Chilli & Chocolate, and Cajun Squirrel—but instead of spending endless amounts running focus groups to learn which flavors were the most promising, Walkers turned the process on its head, simply letting *participation drive production*. The result is nascent responsiveness: like Threadless, Walkers is putting outside-in knowledge in the drivers' seat, rewiring how decisions are made. Walkers's contest was a one-off, but it raises the question: will the next-generation

Walkers resemble Threadless, where democracy is always in charge, surfacing new flavors of chips that satisfy demand reflexively, automatically, and nearly effortlessly? If the economic benefits are as great as they have been for Threadless, the answer might surprise Walkers and the rest of the snack makers of the universe.

Participation is the easiest step on the path to democracy. In fact, the only block to participative decision making is mental. Voting mechanisms are, in a hyperconnected age, too inexpensive for nearly any firm to hesitate about and the benefits too significant to ignore.

So here's a general rule for participation: *whoever is affected by the firm's actions should have the right to participate, with preference given to those affected most.* Only by giving those who are affected most the right to participate can firms identify, monitor, and accumulate the most reliable, consistent, and rapid information about which actions are the most authentically value creating in the first place.

Deliberation

What happens once people have the right to participate? What are they participating *in?* Voting is the most brittle kind of democracy, built on the tiniest kind of conversation, because it limits a voice to a vote. The voting that takes place at Threadless and Walkers is brittle because it can only compress so much knowledge and information into a single number. It doesn't reveal *reasons* for preferred features and attributes, helping people to resolve differing perspectives.

So a deeper kind of democracy is built on *deliberation:* reasoned conversation that details and debates trade-offs between parties with conflicting interests. Deeper than voting, deliberation is rich with information and knowledge. It allows participants to unpack and detail the differing rationales and perspectives that lead to different votes in the first place.

Let's start with what deliberation *isn't:* the anonymous comments sections of newspapers, magazines, and blogs. They're filled to the brim with the linguistic equivalent of drive-by shootings. They're less a Greek forum than a Wild West saloon. Deliberation, in contrast, demands moderation and guidance.

Consider, in contrast, Starbucks. As usual, industrial era business led Starbucks deeply astray, guiding it to build too many stores, expand into too many markets, and dilute the quality of its coffee. But twenty-first-century cornerstones are slowly righting these tremendous errors. Foremost among them is a value conversation. At mystarbucksidea.com, launched in 2008, anyone can participate in Starbucks's decisions by contributing new ideas and voting on others' ideas. Here, Starbucks encourages discussion, context, and exploration, preventing drive-bys by placing ideas under review and moderating discussions. Deeper than mere voting, the deliberation that takes place at mystarbucksidea.com lets the pros and cons of ideas be shared, explained, and debated in detail.

The point isn't that mystarbucksidea.com will *unleash* Starbucks's next radical innovation. Rather, the point is that it *is* Starbucks next radical innovation: it powers managerial agility for Starbucks by radically dropping the cost of making better managerial decisions. Mystarbucksidea.com is already making Starbucks more responsive than rivals. Only a year in, after more than seventy thousand ideas were submitted, Starbucks decided to turn ninety-four of the ideas into reality: a splash stick that fits into the lid of Starbucks cups, a VIP card, and Starbucks VIA Ready Brew, to name just a few. The splash stick didn't do so well, but VIA has taken off. Starbucks is rolling it out globally, expecting to generate more than $1 billion in sales. VIA is in the nascent stages of creating a new category: premium instant coffee. That's thicker value, a better deal for all: customers get what matters to them—and Starbucks, almost for *free*, gets a billion-dollar idea (Hey, Starbucks—where's your stock options plan for *external* innovators?).

Yet to focus on the success or failure of the ideas themselves is to miss the point. Starbucks's real advantage is now being *consistently* able to roll out *better* ideas with *less* effort. A thimbleful will be billion-dollar hits, like VIA, and many will be misses, but through the deliberation of people passionately opposed to and for each, Starbucks has better information faster to gauge whether *all* are duds or not—and when they are duds, better new ideas to replace them with. As Starbucks has discovered, deliberative democracy is a new foundation for a twenty-first-century business, built for more agile decision making, where your customers might just help create your next billion-dollar blockbuster because it's what matters most to them. Now that's thick value.

Association

In the king's court, the king is generally told what he wants to hear. So it is in boardrooms and trading floors alike, where groupthink leads to error after error. Authentic democracy demands participation and deliberation, but it also demands public spaces that are unencumbered and unencroached upon by vested interests, for conversations to ignite. Public spaces allow participants the freedom to deliberate without the fear of retribution, retaliation, escalation, or withdrawal, whether from managers or other participants. Just as deliberation deepens voting, so public spaces are what let the most deliberative conversations happen.

What's the world's most associative organization? Wikipedia just might be a contender. Most publishers take months to make decisions. Yet, like Threadless, Wikipedia hums away with decisions every second of every day, making better decisions faster. Agile decision making is powered by voting at Threadless, but at Wikipedia, deep deliberation takes place, a kind of always-on negotiation among contributors, editors, and administrators. There, simple one-sentence or even one-word contributions and edits are discussed in painstaking, obsessive detail. Are they improvements on what existed already? Do they represent some reasonably impartial point of view? Do they add new knowledge, information, or context? All these questions are fleshed out and hashed out. Anyone can join the deliberation, and anyone is free to leave the deliberation.

So what makes deliberation at Wikipedia so intense? The freedom to associate. At Wikipedia, anyone can become a contributor, editor, or administrator—and anyone can associate with any other contributor, editor, or administrator. The result is a vast public space, open for deliberation's intense conversations. No corporation in the world works that way. That's why no corporation was able to build a Wikipedia.

Wikipedia is radically transparent: every comment, question, and deleted contribution is recorded for future reference and historical accuracy. Anyone can page through not just nearly every Wikipedia edit and entry ever made, but also the discussions and negotiations surrounding them. Transparency builds credibility and attracts voluntary effort. And though there's a tendency among the old guard to dismiss Wikipedia as an error-ridden dumping ground, *Nature*, perhaps the world's preeminent scientific journal, found that Wikipedia's accuracy was comparable to the venerable Encyclopedia Britannica.[6] Wikipedia's approach might be described thus, "By keeping a public record of deliberation, we give you the power to associate freely with us, and any of our editors or administrators."

Ah, come on, Wikipedia. That's just digital socialism. Most corporations can never get as totally transparent and associative as Wikipedia. Right? Think again. Here's an example of the power of association in one of the most opaque industries in the world: food.

At findthefarmer.com—an initiative launched by flour company Stone-Buhr and inspired by journalism professor

and passionate food critic Michael Pollan—people can discover, learn about, and connect with the specific family farms that produced the flour they're baking with. Findthefarmer. com lets anyone and everyone track down the family farm where the wheat in the bag of flour they've just bought was grown and harvested. They can digitally meet the farmer, read the history of how long the family has been farming and why and how they farm sustainably, and see videos of the farm in action. That's the freedom to associate brought to life: Stone-Buhr is giving everyone the tools to associate with its farmers and actively encouraging them to do so.

Stone-Buhr has a long way to go before it "pays off" like Wikipedia has done, disrupting an industry. But here's why it just might. Through the power of assocation, the company is building a food business that is responsive. It's like getting to know your local farmer. Stone-Buhr is effectively saying: we have nothing to hide, and everything to gain, from people associating with farmers, so they can learn about how clean, family-friendly, and green our supply chain is. If there are shortcomings, help us discover them—and help us address them. It's a far cry from Big Food's opaque supply chains. There, you can't deliberate, vote, or associate with farmers and food producers, because Big Food is less interested in responsiveness than push marketing. Talk about thin value. Stone-Buhr, in contrast, is building a twenty-first-century business: the more its customers and farmers associate, the better information it has to make more accurate decisions about how to create value for both, and the stronger incentives it has to stay clean and green. Now that's thick value.

The principle is what's important. Findthefarmer.com, Wikipedia, and mystarbucksidea.com must remain first and foremost public spaces, uncensored save for language and unencumbered by managerial fiat, for association and deliberation to happen. Imagine an economy powered by organizations whose stakeholders are all associating, deliberating, and participating in public spaces. That's the kind of deep democracy twenty-first-century businesses, and perhaps even entire economies, are built on.

Dissent

The fourth pillar of democracy is the right to dissent, granting at some meaningful level the power to veto features, attributes, products or services, and entire businesses. Yes, veto power: the power to veto features, attributes, products, services, and entire businesses.

Veto isn't just "not buying" a product or service. It's *preventing* a product or service from being made: vetoing the *decisions* behind the product or service so resources aren't squandered but are instead allocated to the most productive uses, thus creating thicker value. It's the hallmark of the most intense kinds of conversations. Many organizations are becoming more and more comfortable with the ideas of participation and deliberation, but few have ventured onto the terra incognita of dissent.

Yet veto is how democracy can produce the most significant economic gains. Few democracies grant *every* participant veto power—yet, I suspect, the power to veto must be

handled more efficiently than it is in today's economy. Consider how veto currently works. Customers vote with their wallets. Seeing slowing growth, investors sell short the firm's shares to signal disagreement with management, destroying shareholder value. Relying on the market to signal dissent means that the costs of veto begin in the hundreds of millions and go up from there. There's a better way: grant coalitions of participants the power to "softly" veto managerial choices—to say no to goods they decide create little value for them. That kind of mechanism is economically hyper-efficient: it brings the cost of veto down from hundreds of millions to mere hundreds.

Veto sounds like the most radical of the four freedoms. Is there any company in the world today that gives participants the right to dissent—to simply block the production, marketing, or retail of goods and services? In fact, they're everywhere. Threadless, of course, gives people the right to simply dissent and vote no.

Here's a richer example. Usually, buyers for powerful, developed countries decide for suppliers in weak, developing countries what they need most, such as new dormitories, new roads, new uniforms. Fair Trade creates room for a negotiated premium between powerful retailers, like Starbucks, and relatively weak producers, like coffee farmers. The producers decide democratically what to do with the funds generated by the premium. They might, for example, decide to invest it in better schools, roads, hospitals, or jointly owned capital equipment. Under Fair Trade, the weaker party has the right to dissent. Coffee farmers, for example, act as a democratically powered coalition, dissenting from investments that don't benefit them. Impoverished suppliers can say, "Don't build us a road, or a new dormitory. We're going to use the premium to build a school, because we need one more." Through dissent, they exert managerial control over their own destinies and, in consequence, over the fortunes of more powerful retailers like Starbucks. Fair Trade lets producers veto yesterday's often unethical managerial decisions that squeezed them instead of benefited them.

But the most powerful example of dissent comes from the least likely innovator. Walmart's value cycle is built on fourteen networks that manage different facets of sustainability. Those networks are composed of academics, think tanks, NGOs, and a broad variety of stakeholders. The decisions the networks make about sustainability measures, standards, and goals aren't Walmart's alone: they are made collaboratively *with* stakeholders who have the power to effectively veto Walmart's own choices. As I've discussed, to drive sustainable fishing, Walmart has included the Marine Stewardship Council in its seafood network. The council, not Walmart, defines measures and standards for certain categories of sustainably harvested fisheries. It holds effective veto power over the Beast of Bentonville itself, the power to block thin value and enforce thick value.

Who would've thought that the most powerful—and most feared—corporation in the world would be building a twenty-first-century organization, one that grants the power of no to environmental activists? But Walmart recognizes that dissent is powerful because it explodes the boundaries

of decision making, and forces an organization to make new decisions that create authentic value for all. By letting people say no, dissent asks us to reconsider and broaden our decisions. By letting producers say no, Fair Trade forces distributors and retailers to consider long-run, more beneficial investment decisions, like building hospitals instead of buying heavy machinery.

Veto can be a double-edged sword. Get its balance wrong, and you end up gridlocked and sclerotic, like the U.S. Senate, where cloture motions have skyrocketed in the last two decades.[7] Yet, just as the Founding Fathers created the Senate to exert a moderating influence, so, ultimately, a conversational consensus is most meaningful when veto restrains. If no one can dissent in a conversation, consensus is an illusion and democracy isn't meaningful. Deciding between two equally bad choices is barely democratic. Vetoing one, on the other hand, to be able to generate better choices to decide between is the essence of authentic democracy. The power of veto is freedom from too costly a consensus and the tyranny of the powerful, the wealthy, or the majority. That is what makes consensus powerful.

Summing Up

Bean counters, welcome to civilization. The future of business isn't more command-and-control tyranny. It's deeper and deeper democracy, because democracy is what makes sluggish organizations disruptively responsive. In short, conversations with people replace propositions about "product."

How deep is your democracy? Here's a quick checklist.

- Can people, communities, and society participate in decision making? Are those *affected most* by your decisions actively encouraged, and perhaps even incentivized, to *participate most* or vice versa?

- Is your democracy deliberative? Do participants explore and discuss contrasting, perhaps conflicting, perspectives to illuminate pros and cons? Do you monitor and moderate the expression of perspectives to guard against drive-bys? Is a voice more than just a vote?

- Can people associate freely in your public spaces? Are those spaces truly associative, where, for example, transparent identities linked to histories spark trust and affiliation? Are *you* associating—or are you just a spectator?

- Does anyone or any group of people in the public spaces you've built have the power of no? Is veto power soft or binding? To what extent does it influence your decision making?

- Finally, *which* decisions do you make democratically? Are decisions about, for example, inputs, outputs, logistics, pricing, and customer service democratic? Or are you giving people, communities, and society a voice, only to tune it out?

Chapter Four

Step Three: Resilience

From Strategy to Philosophy

OU'VE MASTERED value conversations and have become as responsive as a finely tuned supercar. The next step in becoming a constructive capitalist is mastering *resilience:* using value conversations and value cycles to attain an evolutionary edge. That's resilience, and it happens by crafting a *philosophy* that emphasizes the first, fundamental principles of value creation, rather planning a *strategy* focused on value extraction.

. . .

How did two nerdy dudes trapped in a computer science department build the world's most iconic brand, the world's

most powerful media company, and perhaps the world's most radical approach to business—all in less than a decade? Here's Google's secret: Larry Page and Sergey Brin's great innovation wasn't more powerful technology. It was more powerful evolution.

Yesterday, "liberation fronts" were movements formed, so their founders would say, to free people from political oppression. Today, they're found on gleaming corporate campuses—to free people from stratego-economic oppression. Nineteen sixty-eight, meet 2009, the year that Google founded a team called—I kid you not—the Data Liberation Front.

The Data Liberation Front's goal is to ensure what geeks call "data portability"—you can take your data with you, anywhere you want, even to rivals' services. Want to switch your manuscript from Google Docs to Word? The Data Liberation Front makes it not just possible, but easy. Want to switch your new book from Word to Google Docs? Sorry, you're out of luck. There's no such thing as a Data Liberation Front at Microsoft, because historically, much to regulators' dismay, Microsoft's goal has been to lock you in, not liberate you. So what's wrong with that? Everything.

Here's how Brian W. Fitzpatrick, DataLib's manager and creator, explains it:

> If we're locking users in, chances are there's no sense of urgency to innovate and make products better. What keeps people coming back to search? Is it because they signed a two-year contract? No way! The reason people

keep coming is it meets their needs best, and we have a team of engineers whose sole job is to keep improving search, so it gets better and better.

You can think of it as a better, new type of lock-in: lock-in through innovation. Yesterday's was based on formats or barriers, like frequent flyer programs: the goal was to create a hostage situation.

Here's an analogy for how we think about it. Let's say I'm a room. I'm not locked in because the doors and windows are sealed shut, but because I have a really comfy seat and a giant plasma TV. Closed systems will get lazy, and complacent. In a room where the doors are locked, and the windows sealed, we don't need comfy seats and big TVs—in fact, we'll take them to another room, where we'll use them to lure people in.

We're not liberating data out of altruism. We're doing it because it makes good business sense, because it drives long-term, sustainable growth.[1]

The impetus for Data Liberation Front came when Fitzpatrick heard Google CEO Eric Schmidt reiterate an important corporate principle: "We don't lock our users in." Fitzpatrick took the idea for Data Liberation Front to Schmidt, who jumped on it: "Why aren't we already doing this?" It was, says Fitzpatrick, "the logical, real-world next step of Googly principles," tracing a line from philosophy to practice.

Listen, though, to Fitz's final lesson, because he's saved the best for last: "Disrupt yourself before someone else comes along and does it. Everyone says someone will come

along and replace Google. We think it should be Google." Now *that's* the beating heart of a resilient organization.

It's counterintuitive, but initiatives like the Data Liberation Front are the real lifeblood of Google's evolutionary edge. Much has been written about Google's experimental approach: rapid, frequent, always-on "bucket" tests in which a baseline product is compared to versions with minor differences, so the "best" product or service can be discovered. But initiatives like DataLib go deeper: they provide the evolutionary pressure that makes Google *keep* experimenting in the first place.

Let me explain with an analogy. A country engaging in protectionism can rarely develop industries and companies that are globally competitive. Its companies, sectors, and industries never face powerful enough incentives because competition is stifled. And so, to ensure free exchange, nations spend countless hours in diplomacy, carving out trade treaties. Though we run the global economy that way, we don't run companies that way, and yet, just as for nations: companies engaging in protectionism can never evolve products, services, and businesses that are authentically better—because incentives to maintain an edge dry up.

So DataLib is the equivalent of an international trade treaty. It says, in effect: "We agree to free exchange—you can take your stuff wherever, whenever you like." And like any international trade treaty, it's an amplifier of evolutionary pressure. It's one of the cogs that compels Google to evolve, setting incentives for it to always offer the best services. Because it exists, you, the user, have the power to say "Man, this is a total fail. I'm moving my stuff to Word"—and so create pressure for Google to evolve. But if you keep your book on Google Docs—well, then it must be better than Word, creating thicker value. In contrast, because Microsoft is always seeking to lock in exchange unfairly, it has dramatically less power to evolve better stuff: if you're held hostage by Microsoft's proprietary .doc family of formats, designed not to work with rival formats, then protectionism is the name of the game. Evolutionary pressure is squelched, and thin value has little impetus to thicken.

So Google's secret sauce isn't just its much-vaunted experimentation, but the *reason* experimentation happens in the first place: Google always seeks free and fair exchange. That means that when something sucks, when no one demands it, when users reject it, then it must fail, and a new product, feature, or attribute must rise in its place. Speed that up, multiply it a thousand times, and you get rapid, consistent experimentation. The end result is resilience: the capability to consistently evolve better stuff faster than rivals, creating thicker and thicker value.

Resilience is applied evolution, and its magic ingredient isn't data, hypotheses, or tests. *Fairness* precedes experimentation in the hierarchy of resilience. Just as air is necessary for human life, so free and fair exchange is a necessary condition to generate an evolutionary edge. Conversely, the price of protectionism, the cost of an unfair advantage, is never evolving stuff that's light years better; the flipside of seeking survival of the quittest is never mastering survival of the fittest.

Consider how different Google's approach is from, for example, Big Food's. If a new product isn't selling well, Big Food's first instinct is to aggressively hypermarket it, pumping up sales in the near term. If a new category appears, Big Food squelches distribution for it by paying off retailers. If a new kind of retailer arises, it quickly locks up prime locations and seals them off. All are ways to stifle free and fair exchange. Because its first instinct is to protect yesterday, instead of simply letting it fail, Big Food has been left totally unable to evolve better stuff at all. Want fries with that thin value?

Big Food's focus is, in other words, value extraction: squeezing farmers, customers, and, when you think about it, society, for as much value as possible. Resilience is its very opposite: the capacity to keep creating thicker and thicker value than rivals.

Every kind of evolution requires selection. Biologists speak of natural selection; sociologists, of social selection. Economic evolution requires *competitive selection*. Customers, buyers, and suppliers must be able to choose freely and fairly between a firm and its rivals, without interference from anyone, anywhere. Free and fair exchange is the bedrock of evolution because it drives competitive selection.

Here's the problem. When organizations put value extraction above value creation, as Big Food does, "competition" isn't. It boils down to a game of what I call economic conflict: unfairly *limiting* and stifling free and fair exchange by threat, intimidation, or pure force. In many, if not most, industries, building an arsenal of anticompetitive moves is business as usual. Trying to gain "survival of the quittest," players seeking an orthodox competitive advantage attempt to limit competition by finding ways to force rivals to quit. The price they pay is that they never evolve *more* competitive products, services, or businesses.

Resilient organizations, instead, are masters of "survival of the fittest." They have the capacity to evolve better stuff faster than rivals by letting the bad stuff fail. Instead of protecting yesterday's uncompetitive business models, products, and services, they expose products, services, and entire businesses to the freest and fairest exchange so they can evolve what is *more* competitive. They are driven by competitive selection. By evolving more and faster than rivals, like Google, they are able to survive and thrive in the fiercest of conditions.

Let's go back to Microsoft. Its Word and Excel programs have barely evolved in a decade. Windows has decayed to the point that many simply refused to upgrade to Vista, a costly disaster. Stagnation is the real price of Microsoft's protectionism, its focus on survival of the quittest, the result of placing value extraction above value creation. Google is the anti-Microsoft: always mutating, changing, and innovating. Yesterday, it was just a search engine. Today, you can search the full text of nearly every book published in the last hundred years at Google Book Search, check your (nearly infinite) e-mail at Gmail, and get your work done anywhere with Google Docs and Spreadsheets. All are evolving a mile a minute because Google doesn't bundle them into Google

search, but forces them, through initiatives like the Data Liberation Front, to stand on their own merits. The goal? Seeking survival of the fittest *against* Microsoft's products. If that process of evolution continues, Google Docs and Spreadsheets will soon be more competitive than stagnant Word and Excel, and Google will once again have made the competition irrelevant.

Resilient organizations create thicker value by evolving stuff that has become radically better. The heartbeat of evolution is rapid, consistent, frequent experimentation—but its lifeblood is free and fair exchange. It is only when exchange is voluntary that an organization can know whether a product, service, or business is creating thin value, and feel the fury of an evolutionary impetus in the first place; it is only when stuff is liberated to compete against rivals, and people are liberated to choose between them, that an organization gains the capacity to evolve—and keep evolving stuff of radically thicker value, gaining an evolutionary edge.

From Strategy to Philosophy

What's the best way to make the competition irrelevant? It's a question that has obsessed generation after generation of strategists, pundits, and gurus. Is it new business models, new market space, harder hardball, or better knowledge? The answer is: none of the above. It's Brian Fitzpatrick's concise summary of Google's great insight: "Disrupt yourself before someone else comes along and does it."

Call it the resilience principle: *disrupt yourself instead of protecting yourself.* If you can, you might just gain the power to evolve thicker value faster—making the competition, still protecting the same old thin value, seem feeble and paltry by comparison. Google boasts an enviable track record of doing exactly that: it's the world's most Darwinian organization, capable of speedier, more consistent evolution—a company that has honed the evolutionary edge of resilience to razor-sharpness. So what gives Google the ability to disrupt itself, for example, to create initiatives like DataLib in the first place?

A radical institutional innovation—a philosophy. Most companies have a competitive strategy, but few have *philosophies.* What's the difference? Night and day. Competitive strategies say, "Here's how we'll get people to buy our stuff, no matter what." A philosophy says, "Here's how we'll make stuff people *want* to buy, no matter what." Competitive strategy is about war on the competition through war on competition *itself:* its goal is limiting free and fair exchange by blocking, deterring, and smashing rivals. But when a company has a philosophy, the tables are turned on war. Companies that have philosophies no longer make war on competition. Like Google, they are able to master a new discipline: they can wage peace instead. They seek freer, fairer exchange, instead of pulling down the iron curtains of protectionism and stifle.

Philosophy is concerned with discovering "first principles"—the fundamental laws that explain the world around us. So it is with organizational philosophies; they

are concerned with discovering, articulating, and living the first principles of value creation—like Google's set of corporate principles. They are fundamental laws that explain how we *won't* merely prevent *others* from creating thick value, but instead how *we* will create, refine, and hone thick value. When an organization specifies how it won't block free and fair exchange, the doors of evolution open, and the result is resilience.

Here's a first principle: Google's now famous "Don't be evil." It prevents Google from merely blocking others, freeing exchange. The result is that Google *must* experiment: don't be evil prevents Google from locking advertisers or customers in, so Google is always tweaking and refining its services, evolving better ones, and gaining resilience. And, to revise that principle a bit: "You can make money without being evil."

Say it fast ten times: first principles force failure. They are what make a company experiment—always, consistently, frequently. *Only* when a company articulates how it *won't* merely block others from creating thick value does the impetus to fail emerge, and the company feels the pressure to evolve products, services, and business that *do* create thicker and thicker value. First principles like don't be evil effectively say, "We never want to threaten, coerce, or manipulate you into using our services. You're free to tell us they suck, by choosing one of our rivals. Please do, because that's the raw horsepower of resilience, the fuel of our evolutionary engine."

How do you discover, articulate, and live your own first principles of value creation? There are two stages in crafting

a philosophy that mirror how the great philosophers under-
stood the world around us: knowing and synthesizing.

Gaining Knowledge

The first stage in crafting any philosophy is *knowing*. For
organizational philosophies, the first stage is knowing conflict: how you are failing to create thick value of your own
and merely preventing *others* from creating it instead. Wherever and however you are taking actions that actively stifle
and limit free and fair exchange, especially in retaliation to
a rival's anticompetitive moves, you are waging war—the
dominant metaphor in business for much of the twentieth
century.

So here's a question that will help diagnose just how
deep your addiction to economic conflict is. How many
of these essential kinds of anti-competitive moves are you
making? How many are the bedrock of the advantages you
depend on?

Collusion and cartels. The most basic way to achieve an
unfair advantage is to corner the supply of a resource. The
textbook example is OPEC, a cartel designed explicitly to
regulate the output of oil. Why has energy investment been
starved for decades? Because when oil prices are too high,
OPEC floods the market, driving prices down. When oil
prices are too low, OPEC starves the market, driving prices
up. OPEC benefits, but people and society are worse off.
Markets cannot price energy scarcity accurately, sending

schizophrenic signals that point boardrooms in conflicting directions. By depending on OPEC's unfair cartel and quota system, and endorsing its regulation of oil supply, oil producers and refiners have underinvested in innovation. The result has been a total failure in the ability of the industry to evolve better, cleaner, and cheaper sources of energy.

Price fixing. When prices are fixed, markets are robbed of information. Consumers and producers alike gain little insight into the relative value of different goods and services, since all prices are the same. In 2008, a trio of LCD manufacturers, including Sharp and LG, pled guilty to fixing prices. They were giving consumers an unfair deal, but they were also giving themselves an unfair deal. By fixing prices, Sharp and LG left themselves unable to discern which LCDs could command a fair premium in the first place. So it's no surprise that they have been notably poor performers in LCDs and, indeed, across markets. The price of playing unfairly was, as always, never learning how to win fairly.

Bid rigging. When bids are rigged, markets break down even more spectacularly, and voluntary exchange becomes nothing short of extortion. The master, of course, was Enron, which implicitly rigged bids. Through anticompetitive tactics and strategies like the aptly named Death Star, Enron gamed California's energy system to receive payments for moving energy and relieving congestion on the grid without actually moving any energy or relieving any congestion. Enron wasn't able to build a better energy industry because it was extracting a profit by manipulating the imperfections in yesterday's industry.

Side payments. In many industries, kickbacks and side payments shape value chains. Remember the not-so-golden days of the dot-com bubble? Back then, investment banks were notorious for laddering: offering shares of upcoming IPOs at a discount to a favored client, which agreed, in turn, to buy more after public trading began, pumping up the share price. Laddering is a side payment that goes both ways: banks at the time offered discounts on megavaluable shares, and favorite customers offered to do more business with banks. Needless to say, everyone not in on the ladder loses.

Similarly, for decades, record labels supplied payola to radio stations and learning how to game the charts to create artificial popularity for their music, because the most popular music was what distributors would take a risk on. As a result, consumers turned off and tuned out an increasingly homogeneous music landscape disconnected from what they really wanted to hear.

Yet side payments are hardly confined to investment banks and radio. Pharmaceutical reps are infamous for giving doctors freebies—from free pens to paid vacations—essentially as side payments to doctors to create incentives for prescribing their drugs. It's a way to achieve "channel control," because doctors are the channel by which drugs get distributed. The result? A dilution of incentives to make better drugs and a threat to the Hippocratic Oath itself.

Bundling and tying. In the eighties, they had two. In the nineties, four. Today, they're up to six and counting. Why do fast-moving consumer goods players keep adding more blades to razors, instead of cooking up a better way to shave? Because, as every aspiring master of the universe knows, the fattest margins are made by tying blades to razors and then making those blades increasingly complex and, hence, increasingly expensive. But what's the long-run result? An arm's race of blade counts. By the time my kids are old enough to shave, razor blades will look like cheese graters. What won't we have? A significantly better shave or shaving experience. It's just another example of orthodox competition's power to limit and stifle evolution and innovation.

Exclusive dealing and refusal to deal. In many industries, players sign noncompetitive deals. I'll let you distribute my goods, if you agree not to distribute any of my rivals' goods. I'll let you retail my widgets, if you agree not to retail any competing widgets. We'll let you produce for us, if you agree not to produce for anyone else. And so on. Never was this truer than in apparel. Brand "orchestrators" orchestrate the production of clothes by marketing, distributing, and sometimes retailing clothes but rarely producing or finishing them. Tommy Hilfiger and Sun Apparel rely on captive suppliers—suppliers made reliant on the sheer order volume that orchestrators can offer.

Thickets. In some industries, players hoard assets they won't use to deliberately exclude others from accessing them. In biotech and health care, players built thickets of patents relating to new diagnostics and therapeutics. The result was that transaction costs across the industry exploded, since each player had to negotiate with numerous others to bring products to market. So biotech never delivered its promise of revolutionizing health care or human wellness.

Division. In some industries, territories or markets are implicitly divided, the unspoken agreement being, "I'll monopolize this, if you let me monopolize that." During the tumultuous years of the dot-com boom, for example, Microsoft made an immodest proposal to the makers of Navigator, the upstart browser then dominating the nascent market. In exchange for Netscape giving up making the Windows 95 version of Navigator, Microsoft would offer a generous cash payment. Microsoft would also implicitly give up making browsers for *other* operating systems. Microsoft was making Netscape an offer to divide up the territory of the browser market: I'll monopolize this operating system, you monopolize that one. If Netscape had agreed, the Internet would likely be a very different place today, one stuck in conflict, stagnation, and devolution.

Synthesizing to Create First Principles

The second stage of crafting a philosophy is synthesizing knowledge to create first principles. It's the same for organizational philosophy. First principles are built by synthesizing

knowledge about the specific kinds of conflict that limit and prevent failure.

First principles specify how *we* will create thick value instead of merely blocking *others* from creating value. They identify specific circumstances in which we *won't* engage in the anticompetitive practices of conflict we have identified as business as usual in our industry, and how we will seek free and fair exchange *instead*. A principle might say: "We won't tie blades to razors. We will make interchangeable razors and blades." Or it might say: "We won't build unproductive, costly patent thickets just to slow the pace of rivals' innovations. We will license unused patents instead." Or it might say: "We won't sign exclusive deals with distributors. We will seek a level playing field for our products instead." Ultimately, first principles express how we will expose our products to free and fair exchange and, in the process, fail, evolve, and become resilient.

Principles are economic trade-offs we're not willing to make. Most businesses are obsessed with "monetization" and business models: what can we sell, and how fast can we sell it? Principles, in contrast, are concerned with what we *won't* sell out. They are not the vague statements of intent that make up most mission statements or values that companies hope to achieve in some utopian future. Rather, they specify actions companies won't take—come hell or high water—because they stop resilience dead in its tracks.

Google is a principle-powered business. It has a now-famous set of corporate principles.

1. Focus on the user and all else will follow.
2. It's best to do one thing really, really well.
3. Fast is better than slow.
4. Democracy on the Web works.
5. You don't need to be at your desk to need an answer.
6. You can make money without doing evil.
7. There's always more information out there.
8. The need for information crosses all borders.
9. You can be serious without a suit.
10. Great just isn't good enough.

The principles are just the tip of a very big iceberg. Google *also* has marketing principles . . . and software principles . . . and design principles. Collectively, all these are Google's "first principles of value creation" that make up its larger philosophy. All specify how Google will create value through free and fair exchange, instead of merely blocking rivals unfairly. These principles are what have let—indeed forced—Google to build a business that fails, evolves, and gains resilience.

Let's use some of Google's principles to do a counterfactual: let's ask how the music and food industries could have been better able to evolve if *they* had had Google's principles.

There's always more information out there. What's the point of Google's "there's always more information out there" principle? To prevent Google from exclusive dealing. Google rarely if ever strikes exclusive deals with advertisers or publishers. Consider the history of the Internet: in the late nineties and

early noughties, rivals signed exclusive revenue-sharing deals with distributors to block competitors. In most cases, vertical integration was the name of the game: AOL bundled access with search and Time Warner's content. Excite partnered with @Home to bundle its content with @Home's fat pipes. The goal? In both cases, to create a walled garden. Instead of letting markets marry the highest-quality content with the lowest-cost distribution, search players worked actively to block competition and limit consumer choice. But because it had no exclusivity to protect, Google sought instead to index all the information it could, instead of hoard only the information it had. The result? Google ended up leading people to the *best* information, where walled gardens led them only to *exclusive* information and content. Today, the "there's always more information out there" principle has exploded product variety: Google has bested its rivals by developing book, academic, and video search. The principle stopped it from engaging in exclusive dealing and let it evolve to index far more information than rivals.

So what might have happened if the music industry had had a "there's always more music out there" principle? Like Google, exclusive dealing would have gone the way of the dinosaur. Instead, record labels would have focused on quality and choice, and a radically more constructive music industry would have emerged. Labels wouldn't have wasted time dickering for a decade over the exclusivity of digital distribution rights, and they probably wouldn't have sued their own customers relentlessly. They would have sought to sign and develop better artists in the first place, experimenting relentlessly with new genres, forms, and delivery methods. Thicker and thicker value.

What would have happened if food retailers had a similar principle? Instead of building land banks to unfairly stifle competition, food retailers would be scouring the globe for the best food, best recipes, freshest ingredients, and most talented chefs. They would be focused on bringing food to market that competitors couldn't match in the first place. "There's always more food out there," and our job is to bring the best and healthiest of it to you. Thick, goopy value.

Democracy on the Web works. What's the point of Google's "democracy on the Web works" principle? Rivals like Ask.com and Excite built businesses on giving advertisers control of vital top-search results, an implicit form of price fixing. You pay a fixed amount; we'll hand search results over to you. The cost, of course, was that relevance for end users plummeted. At rival search engines, variety and choice were limited by payment for results. Google's principles forced Google to compete and never compromise the quality of its search results. "Democracy on the Web works" also means that "payment for search results doesn't." The result was that Google search was forced to be maximally relevant to the user, rather than paid by the advertiser to become less relevant.

What would have happened if the record labels and food manufacturers had a democracy-works principle? Neither

would have built elaborate webs of side payments to retailers in exchange for stocking their products. They would have said, "Let consumers vote with their wallets, because democracy works." Instead of seeking to limit competition, they would have been forced to learn how to produce food and music so much better that retailers *had* to stock it. With a democracy-works principle, food and music players would have exploded the voluntariness of exchange, instead of distorting consumer choice by limiting access to retailers. By doing so, they would have been better able to discover music and food that was meaningfully better in the first place. They would have been more resilient businesses, built on thicker value.

Fast is better than slow. Here's perhaps Google's most revolutionary principle: "fast is better than slow." As Google's Web site announces, "Google may be the only company in the world whose stated goal is to have users leave its website as quickly as possible." How's that for revolutionary? Yahoo!, in contrast, bundled search with horoscopes, music, gossip, and news. The goal? To keep visits as long as possible, even if they didn't benefit consumers, so it could control the ad market by limiting the variety of places to which ads could be distributed. Yet, by *not* forcing people to stick around, Google forced itself to always offer the best services. People flocked to better Google e-mail, search, and video services, and the more people voluntarily utilized Google services, the more Google learned about the information people really wanted.

The end game? Google's ad relevance skyrocketed to three to five times Yahoo!'s, powering Google's ascendance—and Yahoo!'s downfall.

"Fast is better than slow" means: "We won't force feed you. We will always ensure you get more for less." What would happen if the music and food industry had the same principle? In the food industry, that principle might say, "We're the only food company in the world that wants you to eat as little as possible." The natural outcome would be fresher, tastier, and healthier food that delivered more nutrients for the buck—instead of a United States of Obesity—and food producers with a larger bottom line per unit. Food, in other words, full of thick value.

In music, the same principle might say, "We're the only record label in the world that wants you to buy as few of our records as possible." Labels would make higher-quality, higher-priced music meant to last, not the disposable megastars that are the result of marketing wars that have sapped the last ounce of vitality and profitability from the industry. Music would be less dependent on superstars, big marketing budgets, and high-volume deals and would be more artistic, creative, and, well, musical, not to mention profitable.

Now *that's* disruptive: a *single* one of Google's principles might lead to revolutionary outcomes for both these troubled industries. By learning how to prosper without economic conflict, both industries would begin learning to create value that is resilient *to* such conflict. All its principles, old and new, focus Google with laserlike intensity on redrawing

the boundaries of competition: they let Google step outside the boundaries of industrial era competition, becoming resilient to it. Where twentieth-century businesses are always waging war, Google is always waging peace.

No company is perfect. The point isn't that Google's principles lead always and irrevocably to absolutely, totally free exchange. Rather, it's that Google does so *more* than competitors do. Industrial era business evolves slowly, painfully, and often not at all, because most incumbents are fighting tooth and nail to block yesterday's stuff from competitive selection. In contrast, Google strives not to unfairly protect its services and businesses *from* competitive selection, even to the point of setting up a Data Liberation Front. It does this, never perfectly, often with great difficulty, sometimes not at all (witness Google's challenges in applying its principles in China). Yet the focus on free and fair exchange, the resulting evolutionary pressure, and the thicker value that evolves makes Google radically different from the monopolists that came before it and those that surround it.

So Google's great innovation wasn't more powerful technology, but more powerful evolution. That's worth saying twice. Its evolutionary power, Google's famously furious experimentation, has a deeper cause. Free and fair exchange is a necessary condition for it to work and to kick-start it *into* work. Without waging peace, Google can never be sure its experiments are yielding valid, accurate, unbiased results and can never feel the pressure to experiment as furiously as it does. Because it was waging peace *first*, Google has been able to evolve services with thicker and thicker value.

Summing Up

The future of advantage is fair, not unfair. Instead of protecting yesterday's business models, products, and services with more and more unfair tactics and strategies, resilient companies expose themselves to maximum free and fair exchange so they can evolve what creates thicker value. They know that the price of unfair, anticompetitive tactics is never evolving stuff that's light-years better, so they consistently choose fairness over force, philosophy over strategy.

How thick is the value that you can evolve? How resilient is your organization? How powerful is your philosophy? Here's a quick checklist:

- There's almost no industry that's free of conflict. Do you understand how, when, and where conflict happens in your industry, systematically and chronically? Which anticompetitive moves are business as usual, hardwired into negotiations, contracts, and perhaps even mental models?

- Have you crafted first principles that will prevent you from engaging in these moves? Just one or two won't do: have you disarmed most of the arsenal, or just made a half-hearted attempt?

- Do those first principles specify precisely and concisely how *you*, like Google, will create value and seek survival of the fittest, instead of merely unfairly blocking *others* from creating value, seeking survival of the quittest?

- Google's principles add up to a philosophy that lets Google fail cheaper, harder, and faster. Do your principles give you the power to fail—consistently, frequently, inexpensively? Do they force you to evolve toward tomorrow, instead of protecting yesterday?

- Google's philosophy *is* its enduring wellspring of value creation. It's what Google believes in, stands for, and lives and breathes. Do your principles add up to a coherent, self-reinforcing philosophy, that's your enduring wellspring of value creation?

Chapter Five

Step Four: Creativity

From Protecting a Marketplace to Completing a Marketplace

NOW YOU'VE CRAFTED a philosophy and become as resilient as a redwood. The next step in becoming a constructive capitalist is mastering *creativity:* using value conversations, value cycles, and philosophies to achieve the economically impossible. Instead of merely protecting marketplaces from rivals, creativity happens by completing them for people, communities, and society.

Here's how innovators from Silicon Valley to South Asia are striving to do so.

. . .

Credit for the poorest of the far-flung global poor, at a *lower* delinquency rate than the rich? Impossible. A new car that costs less than a midrange mountain bike? Impossible. Electric cars for free? Impossible. Soap and shampoos that end up making the poorest *richer*? Mega-impossible. The full-blown Internet with no corners cut, on your mobile ph . . . scratch that. *More* than the full-blown Internet, on your mobile phone? All 100 percent impossible, right? But that's exactly what constructive capitalism's radical innovators have been busy reinventing, reconceiving, and redefining by rethinking creativity for the twenty-first century.

In most boardrooms, the word *creative* refers to the bespectacled hipsters who make glitzy ads. Under the rules of industrial era capitalism, we're confined to think of creativity as aesthetic or artistic. Yet creativity is economic, too. Bringing new economic arenas into being is a deeply creative act. That economic creativity is ultimately a powerful source of competitive superiority.

Creativity—the third source of constructive advantage—is the apogee of next-generation *productivity.* Industrial age productivity has a simple—and simplistic—definition of it: can we produce more outputs from a given set of inputs? Quantity—not quality—is its measure. In the auto industry, for example, productivity is often measured using workers or labor hours per vehicle. The result? A focus on churning out more cars per worker, not radically better cars per worker.

That's why twentieth-century productivity is a poor match for twenty-first-century economics. In a hypercompetitive world, entry barriers have fallen, product life cycles are compressing, and yesterday's industries, markets, and segments are packed to the brim, boiling with rivalry— and so the ability to churn out even more widgets than the next guy is just another path to commoditization.

Yet, most of us are caught fast there. In most boardrooms, the word *creative* refers to the bespectacled hipsters who make glitzy ads. Under the rules of orthodox capitalism, you've probably been confined to think of creativity as aesthetic or artistic. Yet there's much more to it than that.

Step back into history for a moment to gain deeper insight into the crux of creativity. In 1413, Filippo Brunelleschi dazzled the world and disoriented his artistic rivals by painting lifelike, three-dimensional perspectives on a two-dimensional canvas. To the people at that time, he had achieved the impossible. And the timeless essence of creativity remains the same as it was in Brunelleschi's day: it is about achieving the impossible. Creativity, as a source of constructive advantage, is the ability to achieve the economically impossible. Like master artists create the aesthetically impossible, so masters of next-generation productivity create the economically impossible.

Constructive capitalism is leaping beyond industrial age productivity, to a better definition of productivity: *socioproductivity*, the ability to create not just more (of the same old) "product," but "impossible" new economic arenas: those that are worth the most to people, communities, society,

and future generations, because value is "impossibly" thick. Socio-productivity means being consistently able to create new industries, markets, categories, and segments that rivals consider "impossible," flabbergasting them because they fly squarely in the face of industrial age logic. Forget churning out more me-too widgets than the next guy: how many new thick-value industries, markets, categories, and segments have you created? For most, the answer is none. The majority of companies have never been able to create *any* new segment, category, or market, let alone one full of thick value. Yet, constructive capitalists like Apple and Tata have mastered next-generation productivity, climbing to its apex.

Tata created an impossible new market for low-cost cars with its revolutionary Nano. Banco Compartamos created an impossible new market for the rural poor in Latin America to access credit. Nintendo revolutionized video games by creating impossible new markets for girls and grandmothers (an "impossible" market for most traditional video execs) with its groundbreaking Wii. Apple revitalized mobile telephony with the impossible iPhone and created an impossible new mobile "apps" industry via the iPhone apps market.

What does achieving the impossible mean, from an economic point of view? Mastering socio-productivity means learning to create markets and industries for those whom orthodox capitalism is *unable* to serve. Twentieth-century organizations are awesome at the incremental: creating *low-need–high-cost* markets, segments, and industries, like

Hummers, McMansions, and expensive lattes. Constructive capitalist revolutionaries are instead awesome at the radical. Creative companies are able to create *ultra-high-need–ultra-low-cost* markets, segments, and industries.

All impossible industries, markets, and categories have two things in common. They didn't just meet existing needs in slightly better ways. They met needs that were *never* met or barely met before—ever. They met those needs not at a significant price premium, but at a point of price equivalence or at a disruptively lower price. The combination of high need with low cost, as figure 5-1 illustrates, underpins economic impossibility.

The Nano is high need. It begins to fulfill the barely met transportation needs of the Indian poor—a thin, patchwork

FIGURE 5-1

Impossible markets

		Well met	Undermet	Never met
Price advantage			Nano Wii GrameenPhone	iPhone Apps Store Wii Google Search
Price equivalence				iPhone
Price disadvantage		Hummer		

Greater economic impossibility

Relative price differential

Low need–High need

semipublic transport network and pricy used cars with steep maintenance costs—at an ultra-low cost. The iPhone is high need: never before was the ability to surf the unadulterated Internet on a mobile phone catered to, a need for information overlooked for decades by orthodox handset makers despite the explosion of Internet usage throughout the nineties and noughties. And while the iPhone sure isn't the cheapest phone on the market, it's priced at par with high-end smartphones from RIM, Nokia, and Motorola. The Wii is high need and relatively low-cost: never before has a video game console been utilized to fulfill the undermet, growing needs for mental and physical fitness in developed countries—the more expensive Xbox 360 and Playstation 3 largely fulfilled the already very well-met need for adrenaline-pumping games for adolescents. What seems impossible to rivals is the one-two punch of meeting never-before-met needs at the same or lower price as they are asking. Just ask Ford, Chrysler, Sony, and Microsoft, which still can't believe just how deeply they are threatened by masters of socio-productivity.

When an organization masters socio-productivity, as Apple, Tata, and Nintendo are taking baby steps toward doing, it gains creativity—the ability to create ultra-high-need–low-cost markets where value is thickest. From an economic point of view, high-cost–low-need markets create thin value because they are concerned with offering diminishing marginal benefits to the already best-off. In contrast—as we will explore—ultra-high-need–low-cost markets create thick value, because the *least well-off* are made the *most better-off*. For GM, the Hummer marquee, so obviously aimed at the opulent that its slogan might as well have been "let them eat cake," was value creating for less than five years. Tata's Nano, on the other hand, promises to power decades of thick value by sparking a new category of ultracompact cars—with greater fuel efficiency than SUVs—globally affordable to the impoverished.

Orthodox rivals, bewildered by economically creative companies that turn the logic of the industrial age upside down, often focus on imitating products and services. Think about how Microsoft imitated the iPod with the Zune, or Sony imitated the Wii with a motion-sensing controller for the PlayStation 3. Yet what these players consistently fail to see is that better products and services *aren't* what constructive capitalists are disrupting them with: creativity is. What they should try to replicate instead is the ability of economic creativity itself and use it to seed their *own* impossible new industries, markets, categories, and segments.

The lesson is that creativity is not a resource, but a *competence*—instead of being a specialized, localized, often ghettoized function, it is a capability woven into the fabric of an organization. So it doesn't just mean creating a handful of flashier new products and services or protecting them with an arsenal of patents, brands, and trademarks. Rather, it means having the *ability to always* strive for a tight definition of what is economically "impossible."

If, a decade ago, I told you that the future of electronics wouldn't be created by Microsoft, Nokia, or Sony, but by *Apple*—you might have asked me: "That's pretty good. Where can I catch the rest of your comedy routine?" Yet, in the short

space of that single decade, a company believed to be on the brink of extinction has upturned no less than *four* industries: music, computing, mobile, and retail. These days, the Fifth Avenue Apple Store might be the world's most profitable retail location in the world.[1] So what's so special about Steve Jobs? It's not *just* that he's made sure Apple's aesthetic creativity is never compromised. More powerfully it's that he's made sure that Apple's *economic* creativity, its mastery of creating new, thicker-value markets and categories never is—by hardwiring it into a new cornerstone.

From Protecting a Marketplace to Completing a Marketplace

Protecting marketplaces is a fundamental cornerstone of industrial era capitalism. Because orthodox productivity requires that companies churn out more of the same widgets than the next guy, all try to protect the same old existing segments, categories, and markets from rivals' encroachment, discovering cleverer ways to block, defeat, and smash them. Yawn. That's contesting the same old thin value.

In stark contrast, constructive capitalists—masters of socio-productivity—create new segments, categories, and markets, and not just any old ones, but those of maximum benefit to people, communities, society, and future generations where value is impossibly thick. They create ultra-high-need–low-cost economic arenas where the least well-off are made the most better-off. How do they do it?

With a radical new cornerstone. Instead of protecting marketplaces, they are completing them. In a complete marketplace, every product and service is available, affordable, accessible, functional, and serviceable to, for, and by all for the same share of relative income. The poor might never be able to afford a Bentley, but in a complete car marketplace, they can at least afford a Nano. Value is thickened because new transportation opportunities for the least well-off emerge. Complete marketplaces make the world a disruptively *fairer* place.

Theoretically, value should thicken and improve to the point where nearly everyone is able to enjoy the products and services offered in an industry, prices relative to income. Competition and innovation should make what was once a luxury a necessity. Capitalism should be an engine of equity. Improvements in the basic dimensions of choice—affordability, accessibility, availability, functionality, and service—should happen consistently, as innovators discover new opportunities to create thicker and thicker value from serving the underserved, whether they are at the bottom, top, or middle of the pyramid.

Who is underserved in a democratic(sure?)

Yet, in practice, capitalism doesn't work that way. Most marketplaces remain incomplete, excluding vast swaths of the world's population and limiting incumbents to thin value. Until Tata came along, not everyone could afford a car. Even now, the Nano remains unaffordable for the world's poorest 2 billion.

Industrial era capitalism is rife with inequities: unwanted disparities in affordability, accessibility, availability,

or service that limit opportunities to consume, produce, or contribute. For constructive capitalists, inequities are like gigantic bull's-eyes, alerting them to the limits of the economically possible, the boundaries of thick value. They say, "Look! Over here! We've hit the point of no improvement. We can't make products and services any more accessible, affordable, available, functional, or serviceable." *Here's* where value can't be thickened anymore.

Listen to how scholar Emma Rothschild describes one of the most unfair inequities: "The poorest fifth of Americans spend 31 percent of their income on transport, compared to 21 percent for the second poorest, 17 percent for the third poorest, 15 percent for the fourth poorest, and 10 percent for the richest Americans."[2] The numbers are saying, "We can't provide low-cost cars. It's impossible. Value has stopped thickening and improving." The global rich had plenty of choice in autos, while the global poor had none. Detroit automakers didn't see the world through the lens of that inequity, so kept on protecting SUVs, defending thin value. But Tata saw the world very differently. It focused on inequity—an incomplete marketplace for autos—like a laser beam. Tata asked, "How can we serve people, communities, and societies that are chronically and consistently underserved, marginalized, or ignored by automakers?" Its simple, world-changing answer was, "What if we can make a low-cost car for the poor?"

Here's another, less obvious, inequity: mobile phone users spend the most for the poorest, most limited, most painfully obtuse Internet access. That's just shorthand for, "We can't provide more than a crippled Web on a mobile phone. It's impossible. Value has stopped thickening and improving." Nokia, Sony, and other handset incumbents didn't see the world through the lens of inequity, so they kept on protecting existing smartphones, guarding thin value. Apple saw the world very differently. It approached that lack of improvement like a hammer hitting a wayward nail. Apple asked, "How can we serve people, communities, and societies that are chronically and consistently underserved, marginalized, or ignored by handset makers?" Its simple, world-changing response was another question, "What if we can make a phone that makes the entire Internet usable for everyone, not just geeks, at the same price as a regular smartphone?"

So you might ask: *why* do marketplaces fail to complete, yielding inequities? Because of economic imperfections. Here's how Ramon DeGennaro, the University of Tennessee's SunTrust Professor of Finance, describes them: "Market imperfections generate costs which interfere with trades that rational individuals make (or would make in the absence of the imperfection)."[3] Economic imperfections, then, limit what we can supply, how we can supply it, or who can demand it. They are obstacles and barriers that prevent improvement and limit and stifle the needs of some or many from ever being served. Poor information, resource unavailability, and steep complexity costs are three common kinds of imperfections. Each stops further improvement from

happening, limiting and stifling how complete a market-place can be.

Think about it this way. If we had infinite, cheap resources and information, and could join them together at no cost, we could probably make pretty much any good affordable, available, and accessible to just about everyone. But if information about what to produce is scarce, the resources to make it are unavailable, and if complexity prevents us from joining its component parts—then the affordability, availability, accessibility of a good must hit a hard stop and will only ever be possible for a few, not all.

Instead of defending existing markets, segments, and categories *from* rivals, constructive capitalists make a different choice: to complete marketplaces *for* people, communities, society, and future generations. Their goal is consistently, rapidly, frequently creating "impossible" new segments, categories, and markets instead, by perfecting imperfections. When the two go head to head, the former disrupts the latter. Impossible markets grow faster and yield steeper returns because they commoditize existing ones.

There's only one thing more powerful than a locked-down fortress of a marketplace: a pathway to perfection that can make a marketplace more complete, unlocking thicker value. Both Apple and Tata were able to perfect a long-standing imperfection: they *simplified complexity.* Both discovered that impossible new industries, markets, and categories pop into existence when economic imperfections that stop and stifle improvements from happening are erased. And what

GM, Chrysler, Sony, and Nokia are learning the hard way is this: *nothing* can offer protection from constructive capitalists who wield the world-changing power of perfection.

Perfecting imperfections begins by seeking inequities, the telltale signs of incomplete markets, and it ends by completing marketplaces with "impossible" new segments, categories, and markets. Orthodox businesses ask, "How can we protect existing markets?" Constructive capitalists ask instead, "How can we complete marketplaces by creating new markets that serve people, communities, and societies chronically and consistently underserved, ignored, or marginalized? Can we *simplify complexity, turn products into assets, subdivide resources, or minimize information costs*—and perfect yesterday's imperfections?"

By asking those questions, constructive capitalists are pioneering four paths to perfection—meta, micro, macro, and ortho. Here's how each leads to the creation of "impossible" new industries, markets, and categories.

Meta

Meta means above and beyond. It has to do with information: what sits above and beyond markets and wires exchanges together. Often, markets remain incomplete because of poor information. The more expensive information is, the more costly transactions are, and the more categories and segments are underserved. There are many flavors of costs associated with poor information: search, monitoring, and

enforcement costs. Where these costs are rife, constructive capitalists are discovering often radical mechanisms that offset and minimize them.

Nowhere is information more problematic than in finance. There, the poor were chronically underserved because monitoring and enforcing debt repayment seemed to be intractable. Until, that is, the microfinancial revolution. Microfinance, pioneered by Muhammad Yunus, was built on an ingenious solution to monitoring and enforcement. Yunus made loans to groups (usually women), which would take collective responsibility for monitoring and enforcing repayment. He slashed information costs by effectively spreading them across villages and local communities. Today, constructive insurgents like Grameen and Banco Compartamos have created an "impossible" new industry—one worth more than $30 billion—where the average loan is less than $100, delinquency rates are less than 5 percent, and margins hover near the 60 percent mark. It is growing at light speed, even while industrial age finance is in a state of turmoil. Now that's thick value.

To get *meta*, ask yourself, can slashing information costs let us serve the chronically underserved, marginalized, or ignored?

Micro

Micro has to do with divisibility. Often, markets remain incomplete because products and services are monolithic: only available in *Titanic*-sized increments, they cannot be subdivided, so they remain inaccessible, unaffordable, or unreachable for many categories and segments. When monolithic products and services make markets imperfect, constructive capitalists are learning to get micro. They are slicing and dicing them up, so that new categories and segments can be ignited.

Equity doesn't just have to do with the poor. Sometimes, it has to do with CEOs and hedge fund managers, too. Even for these masters of the universe, a private jet was often out of reach. Heartbreaking, right? By slicing and dicing up the ownership of planes, the now-famous NetJets created an "impossible" new market, where any penny-ante millionaire can own a fraction of every billionaire's favorite plaything. Because private jets spend significant amounts of time idle, fractional ownership was a powerful way to explode affordability. Yesterday, jets were indivisible: today, with the Marquis Jet Card, anyone can buy even a twenty-five-hour microchunk of a private NetJet. That will run you just over $400,000 on a Gulfstream V, which might sound expensive—unless, of course, you've got a spare $35 million or so for a new one. Now there's a price advantage.

Zipcar, of course, did to cars what NetJets and its cousins did to airplanes. But there's an even more radical example of getting micro in autos. Better Place is building an electric power grid and infrastructure for next-generation cars where you can recharge your electric car or swap out a worn-out battery. It's planning on pricing cars like cellular data: on miles plans. You'll be able to pay fixed or variable rates for miles that reflect energy prices. Or you can choose

an all-you-can-eat, flat-rate plan for unlimited miles. Standard electric car batteries cost between $10,000 and $20,000. They are a monolithic, fixed expense. But Better Place makes that expense "micro." It is essentially selling subscribers microchunks of batteries—or macrochunks of batteries, if you buy the flat-rate plan—by selling them miles instead. As Better Place's vice president of Auto Alliances, Sidney Goodman, explained to the *Wired* Autopia blog, "We're an electrical services provider . . . we buy batteries and electricity, and we sell miles."[4] Better Place is making the fixed expense of an electric car battery micro by dividing batteries across subscribers. Here's the kicker: if you subscribe to enough renewably powered miles, you'll get the car for *free*. The model holds enough profit potential that Better Place plans to subsidize cars with miles, just as mobile operators subsidize phones with minutes.

Who else has gotten micro? Apple—with the iPhone Apps Store. Yesterday, mobile services were parts of larger, monolithic subscriptions. Today, at the Apps Store, there are an endless number, and most cost less than a latte. By turning mobile services micro, Apple redrew the boundaries of availability—at last count, more than a hundred thousand apps were on offer.

The master of micro, of course, is Twitter. Yesterday, media were monolithic: newspapers, books, films—all indivisible, costly, and limited in availability. Today, media have been atomized, blown into atomic microchunks—like blog posts, YouTube videos, and tracks to download. The most miniscule of these microchunks? Tweets—just 140 characters of text are all you're allowed. Twitter's secret was this: founders Evan Williams, Biz Stone, and Jack Dorsey realized that microchunks of media could redraw the boundaries of information availability and accessibility, letting people contribute, read, share, and engage with one another more efficiently. How much more efficiently? By getting micro, Twitter might just be beginning to turn search and communication upside down. It's often said that imitation is the sincerest form of flattery—and in early 2010, after admitting that Twitter is what people are turning to for real-time search, the mighty Google began to include tweets in its own search results.

To get *micro,* ask yourself: does dividing, subdividing, or microchunking monolithic, indivisible products and services let us serve the chronically underserved, marginalized, or ignored?

Macro

Macro has to do with turning products and services into assets. Sometimes, markets remain incomplete because the assets that underpin production and consumption aren't tradable or are nonexistent in the first place—assets like knowledge, suppliers, distribution networks, or cash. When markets remain imperfect because the asset infrastructure they need to thrive is missing, constructive capitalists are learning to get macro by selling not mere products and services, but what you might call "businesses in a box."

Grameen, the microfinancial revolutionary, went on to jointly pioneer a mobile phone service—Grameenphone, today Bangladesh's top mobile operator—with 40 percent market share. Yet, the last thing Grameenphone is doing is dominating the same old market. It has displaced rivals by creating a radically more complete marketplace for telephony, consisting of several new categories and segments. Here's one example.

Grameenphone's revolutionary Village Phone service turns mobile phones macro: from products into assets. It provides the poor with microfinancing of up to $200 to finance a phone and training to rent it out for individual calls in their towns and villages. Phones become *assets* that power enduring, lasting gains—not merely products to be consumed. So Village Phone doesn't sell phones: it finances the loans to micro-entrepreneurs of a "business in a box," and those micro-entrepreneurs are no longer consumers; they are Village Phone Operators. The micro-businesses they run create thick value that accrues to themselves, mobile networks, microfinancial institutions—and to their communities, and society alike. Now *that's* authentic, meaningful, enduring thick value. As mobile phones become more ubiquitous and micro-entrepreneurs prosper, Village Phone Operators can become Village Phone network operators, or perhaps even Village laptop officers.

Yesterday, Hindustan Unilever was in the fast-moving consumer goods (FMCG) business. Today, it's in the fast-moving consumer *assets* business via its radical Shakti initiative. After struggling with the complexities of the minimum efficient scale necessary to reach the rural poor, Hindustan Unilever decided to try something totally radical. In fifty villages in 2002, in partnership with NGOs, banks, and local governments, Unilever gave poor rural Indian women microloans, entrepreneurial training, and access to buy its goods wholesale. The idea? To turn consumer goods into assets. Shakti participants aren't consumers; they are micro-entrepreneurs who have, like Village Phone Operators, gained a business in a box—an FMCG distribution business, complete with inventory, training, and working capital.

The result? Today, there over forty-five thousand Shakti entrepreneurs. Unilever has extended its rural reach by north of 30 percent, at significantly lower cost than building industrial age distribution channels. Shakti is so successful that Unilever is applying the initiative across emerging markets globally. It has already kicked off in Sri Lanka and Bangladesh. On average, Shakti participants double their incomes. For the poorest of the poor, that's a life-changing result that creates not just financial wealth, but dignity and self-esteem. Rojamma, a Shakti participant, says: "Today everyone knows me. I am someone now."[5] People win, society wins, and Unilever wins. Everyone prospers. It's a moving example of thick value.

To get *macro,* ask yourself, can turning products and services into assets let us serve the chronically underserved, marginalized, or ignored?

Ortho

Ortho has to do with simplifying complexity. Ortho means *straight,* or *straightforward.* Markets often remain incomplete because complexity imposes steep costs on production and consumption, rendering products and services uneconomical for many potential buyers, suppliers, or customers.

Imagine if you could do everything in your life by pressing a single button. Sounds absurd, right? Not to Steve Jobs. That's Apple's goal: one button to rule them all. Consider for a second just how close the iPhone gets to achieving it. Where most phones have a billion buttons, switches, and doodads, the iPhone has just . . . a single button. The real secret of Apple's success is radical simplicity: stripping every last unnecessary step out of each and every process customers must undertake, which makes products and services usable to the point of surprise, delight, and amazement. Like all of Apple's products, the iPhone is revolutionary not just because it's a better gadget, but, more deeply, because it's an astonishingly simpler gadget.

Apple's revolutionary gestural software made browsing the Web simple enough for everyone. And its seamless sign-up process makes buying and activating an iPhone painless. There's no profusion of plans designed to cow consumers into submission by confusion. That focus on simplicity carries through to billing, where consumers aren't plagued with the hidden charges that mobile operators are infamous for: they see one flat monthly subscription fee. And, of course, in combination with iTunes and the iPhone Apps Store, the iPhone and iPod are doubly revolutionary, because the processes of finding, selecting, downloading, and consuming media and apps are made vastly simpler. Navigating devices like mobile phones and MP3 players used to be an exercise in complexity so costly that most features ended up being unused and the assets mobile players invested—like the mobile Internet—crashed and burned. The iPod, iTunes, iPhone, and the Apps Store, in stark contrast, suck *out* complexity by dramatically reducing the number of steps necessary to achieve goals. By simplifying the complex, to thicken up thin value, Apple creates new markets—and revitalizes dead ones—with a pace that leaves rivals reeling.

Tata is from the other side of the world, yet, strategically, it's like Apple's long-lost brother. How did Tata create the world's first low-cost car? Through the revolutionary power of simplicity. Power windows, power steering, power door locks, air-conditioning? None of these are included in the basic model. The body is made partly of plastic. Adhesive and plastic joints are what hold it together, not welding. The Nano is a twenty-first-century Model T, radically stripped down to just the essentials to radically bring down the price. Even the wheels have just three nuts and bolts holding them in place, instead of the usual four. Great fodder for late-night comics, to be sure. But also a great disruption for Detroit automakers, which, instead of creating impossible new markets through radical simplicity, kept on protecting yesterday's markets by pumping out the same old gas-guzzling, thin-value-creating SUVs. The Nano, in contrast, not only gets better mileage than an SUV, but also makes

those who are less well off the most better-off, leading to thicker value.

To get *ortho,* ask yourself, can simplifying complexity let us serve the chronically underserved, marginalized, or ignored?

Summing Up

Striving to push equity past its accepted limits—perfecting imperfect marketplaces, instead of merely protecting them—is what lets constructive capitalists like Tata and Apple create "impossible" new markets, segments, and industries. When we strive for equity, we refuse to accept the status quo of in-equity and challenge it by saying yes. Yes, we can serve those people. Yes, we can offer that community our products. Yes, we can make our services accessible to those customers. Yes, we can solve that problem. Here's how we *can* improve and create thicker value.

The fount of economic creativity is the refusal to accept the boundaries of the possible, and it is inequities that signal its limits. Here's a quick checklist to kick-start your thinking.

- Are you fighting ever-fiercer battles to protect and shield existing markets and customers from competitors? Instead, can you create new industries, markets, categories, and segments—especially those that are "impossible" in the eyes of the status quo?

- Can simplifying the complex let you serve the under-served, marginalized, or ignored? If you were to simplify the complex, which dimension of inequity—affordability, accessibility, and availability, or functionality and service—could be improved?

- Can microchunking and dividing the mono-lithic let you serve the underserved? If you were to microchunk and divide fixed assets, which dimensions of inequity could you enhance?

- Can turning products and services into assets let you serve the underserved? If you were to offer assets instead of products and services—perhaps even a "business in a box"—which dimensions of inequity might be bettered?

- Can slashing information costs—like negotiation, monitoring, and enforcement costs—let you serve the underserved? If you were to slash information costs, which dimensions of inequity could you upgrade?

- Which new economic arenas could you create by improving affordability, accessibility, and availability, or functionality and service? In your industry, along which dimensions are further improvements consid-ered to be literally "impossible"?

Chapter Six

Step Five:
Difference

From Goods
to Betters

Y LEARNING the art of marketplace perfection, you've become as creative as Picasso. The next step in becoming a constructive capitalist is mastering *difference*: using value conversations, value cycles, philosophies, and creativity to make a meaningful difference, that matters in human terms. Instead of just producing goods, a constructive capitalist makes *betters*—bundles of products and services that make a difference to people, communities, and society by having a tangible, meaningful, enduring positive impact on them.

What do betters look like? Let's go to the videotape.

. . .

It was one of the most iconic products of the twentieth century—branded with the endorsement of the world's coolest athlete, megamarketed at Super Bowls and in sporting magazines, priced just out of the reach of the masses. Every pimply teenager wanted a pair—and so did every competitor. Air Jordans helped turn Nike into the behemoth it is today.

So you'd think Nike would keep on keepin' on. Why then is the twenty-first-century Nike doing an abrupt volte-face? Why is it helping every customer master the discipline of becoming a better runner, instead of—as yesterday—merely persuading people to wear cooler shoes?

The answer: because Nike is just one of the constructive capitalists discovering that, in the twenty-first century, the most disruptive, profitable, and valuable path to advantage isn't *differentiating* stuff, but *making a difference* to people, communities, and society.

Industrial era business isn't just economically unsustainable. It's also strategically unsustainable. Why? Because it faces a tremendous strategic conflict of interest with people, communities, society, the natural world, and future generations. The overriding goal of an industrial business is, as long as it is profitable, to push more at people, whether it makes them better off—or worse off.

Those incentives are deeply at odds with postmodern society's Prozac-flavored problem: what you might call happiness scarcity. Though incomes have grown, the amount of happiness in developing countries has hit diminishing returns.[1] According to the National Opinion Research Center's General Social Survey, happiness in the United States has fallen. The percentage of very happy people peaked in the early 1970s at 38 percent and has fallen to 32 percent since. Never has it risen above 40 percent. In the eight core EU countries, happiness levels have stayed flat, rising by less than 1 percent over the last thirty years, according to the Eurobarometer survey. In Japan, the Cabinet Office's "National Survey on Lifestyle Preferences" reports that the percentage of "very happy" people has dropped precipitously, from 10 percent in 1978 to less than 6 percent in 2005, though GDP more than doubled over the same period. In China, according to the World Values Survey, the percentage of "very happy" people declined from nearly 30 percent in 1990 to about 20 percent in 2008.

Richard Easterlin, a pioneering happiness economist at the University of Southern California, offers the following conclusion: "Over the long term, happiness and income are unrelated."[2] There is debate among economists about such a hard-line view—what's known today as the Easterlin Paradox. The middle ground suggests that though there is, as you might suspect, a link between income and happiness, it's a relationship that diminishes rapidly. Even the richest economies in the world, as rich as they might get, cannot seem to offer more than 40 percent to 50 percent of their members the opportunity to maximize their happiness and become "very satisfied."

Diminishing returns to happiness suggest that for every dollar, pound, or yen of income we earn, we are realizing tiny, incremental gains to happiness, and in some cases, we are becoming *less* happy. When economies—and corporations—play by twentieth-century capitalism's rules, it seems that happiness ends up, ultimately, resembling a zero-sum game. Though we may earn more, total happiness is at worst stagnant—or, at best, multiplies at only a glacial pace. It's as if when we feel happy, it's because increments of happiness are simply transferred from one person to another and then back again, or, worse, because we are borrowing happiness from our future selves. Here, then, is my suggestion; capitalism as we know it has hit a glass ceiling of happiness—a limit to the amount of happiness and very happy people its cornerstones can create in the long run.

The results of research into *what* makes people happiest—and unhappiest—are telling. According to the work of eminent London School of Economics economist Richard Layard, we're happiest when we're relaxing, socializing, or—you guessed it—having sex. The three most unhappy activities his research reveals? The commute *to* work, time *at* work, and the commute back *from* work.[3] Who are the people we are most—and least—happy interacting with? Friends and family make us happiest. Clients and customers make us the third most unhappy. Being alone makes us the second most unhappy. What's at the very, very bottom of the list? Even worse than being alone? Having to interact with your boss.

Dilbert, take a bow.

The problem, I suggest, is this: industrial era organizations were built to profit by producing, marketing, distributing, and selling as much stuff as possible. And though many have urged business to shift away from raw "product" (like Joe Pine and Jim Gilmore's notion of an "experience economy,") none have made the leap to what just might shatter the glass ceiling of happiness.[4]

Happiness doesn't depend on more stuff, but on better *well-being*. Though we may consume more industrial age stuff, the human outcomes that make us happier—like connectedness, economic security, and healthfulness—aren't enhanced. At the limit, they are actually degraded. Obesity, stagnating wages for the middle class, the loss of trust, all these predict a steep fall in tomorrow's happiness. Never mind the industrial era corporation is built to keep pushing out the "product" that results in these negative outcomes, even when it destroys tomorrow's happiness and limits today's.

The thickest, most authentic kind of value—that matters to people, communities, and society in human terms—is value that reflects lasting, tangible gains to happiness. An economy composed of organizations profiting by making people *less* happy—marginally or absolutely—meets the deepest definition of unsustainability. It is built on the very definition of thin value. Profit, business value, or shareholder value that makes us unhappy isn't valuable to anyone but a masochist.

So the most significant—and most vexing—question twentieth-century business faces in the twenty-first century

is: can we redraw the boundaries of happiness? There appears to be a broad limit to the number of "very happy" or "very satisfied" people, under the rules of industrial age capitalism, that even the richest countries can consistently reach. Can we, just maybe, build companies—and ultimately countries and economies—that have new muscles and sinews, strong enough to shatter this glass ceiling of happiness?

Today's innovators might just be doing exactly that—by seeking *difference* instead of mere *differentiation.* In the industrial era, firms sought to differentiate products and services. The name of the game was adding perceived value through more elaborate brands, cleverer slogans, or more gripping ads. Difference, in contrast, is not about how differentiated our stuff is, but whether we can *make a difference* to people, communities, society, and future generations.

Difference stems from mastering next-generation effectiveness: *socio-effectiveness.* It's radically different from capitalism's definition of effectiveness: operating effectiveness. Here's how eminent management thinker Michael Hammer famously described operating effectiveness two decades ago: not merely "doing things right," but "doing the right things."[5] Wasted operations were discarded, and the operations retained were squeezed to get the most bang for the buck. Three sigma became six sigma became nine sigma. Result? Product quality skyrocketed, inventories plummeted, and product life cycles compressed. Operational effectiveness has to do with *outputs:* how consistently, reliably, and frequently inputs turn into good or error-free outputs.

So how does this translate — example? (handwritten)

Socio-effectiveness has to do not with the goodness of outputs, but the goodness of *outcomes.* It isn't about doing things right or doing the right things. It is about *righting the things we do*—ensuring that our products and services ultimately result in positive, tangible benefits and refraining from those that don't, can't, and won't. Socio-effectiveness is measured by how consistently, reliably, and frequently our outputs—which are just inert objects, raw stuff—actually translate into tangible, positive outcomes.

Here's why righting the things we do matters. Outputs are what organizations *produce,* and mastering operational effectiveness has made most companies great at making stuff. But outcomes are what happen *after* what they produce is consumed. But what happens as the ultimate consequence of production, long past the point of consumption? Does doing business with them create tangible, positive outcomes for anyone else, whether customers, communities, society, or future generations? Unless they do, the thickest value can never fully accrue.

Though operational effectiveness has increased dramatically, it seems that socio-effectiveness hasn't and, in many cases, has gone into reverse. How consistently, frequently, and reliably can a given organization make people tangibly better off? Do our cars, food, software, and credit cards actually go on to make a positive difference? Too often, the answer is no. The industrial economy is full of food that makes people unhealthier, communications and interactions that destroy social connections, and financial mechanisms that, of course, have destroyed an unparalleled amount of wealth.

145

As individuals, organizations, and collectively as a larger economy, we are chronically deficient at ensuring positive outcomes. That's no surprise. The outcomes of people, communities, society, and future generations are omitted entirely from the economic fundamentals of industrial era capitalism and so are absent from organizational and managerial decision making. The result? Industrial era business is free to create thin value because profits can be booked by selling people differentiated product—with little regard for whether they are made better or worse off in the long run.

Difference requires that we do something larger, more significant, and more vital than merely differentiate the same old stuff. It requires us to ensure we are making a *real economic difference.* When an organization masters socio-effectiveness, it has more tangible, positive outcomes than rivals do, making a difference in human terms, not just merely offering superficially differentiated products and services. Difference, by itself, may not be sufficient to endlessly boost happiness upward, but I'd argue that today it is *necessary* to create new net happiness for people, communities, society, and future generations to enjoy. So those who can make a difference are developing the muscles and sinews to, at long last, break the industrial age's glass ceiling of happiness.

And through that ceiling lies a new level of advantage. Striving to make a difference isn't about altruism, charity, or philanthropy: in fact, it's about their very opposite, *strengthening* the hammer of strategy. When a company focuses on happiness, the great conflict of interest between industrial-era business—premised on selling more outputs—and people, communities, and society—made better off only by gains to well-being, vanishes—and becomes a *shared* interest in better outcomes instead. Hence, businesses that can make a difference are already realizing greater loyalty, credibility, and legitimacy than rivals because they offer people, communities, society, the natural world, and future generations not a conflict of interest, but instead the thickest, most authentic value.

In the twenty-first century, businesses that can't make a difference are already becoming extinct. In contrast, radical innovators like Nike and others that are learning to make a difference are thriving. In fact, they are redefining *why* business is in business.

From Goods to Betters

Profit, growth, and shareholder value aren't ends in themselves; they are rewards for making others tangibly, durably better off in ways that matter to them the most. If we're profiting, growing, or creating shareholder value, but the *well-being* of people, communities, society, or future generations isn't consistently, accurately enhanced, what we're doing isn't economically meaningful. It has no economic significance, because no authentic economic value has been created. Alone, chasing profit, growth, and shareholder value is a meaningless recipe for creating thin value, whose debt catches up with every company sooner rather than later.

And increasingly, what we're doing *isn't* economically meaningful. That's what happiness scarcity is shouting out from every SUV, Big Mac, and McMansion. Raw stuff becomes economically meaningful *only* when it actively affects people's well-being positively. Do you make video games that amplify people's relationships more than others, shoes that help keep people fitter than others, or laptops that make people more productive than others? Are people smarter, fitter, healthier, or more connected as a result of interacting with your business? That is the truest and hardest test of authentic value creation.

"Some people have trouble playing the positioning game because they are hung up on words. They assume, incorrectly, that words have meanings." That's the advice that Al Ries and Jack Trout famously dispensed to boardrooms thirty years ago in their classic book, *Positioning.*[6] The result was indeed "words without meanings." See this can of beer? It's going to help you meet more beautiful women. In reality, the beer is a mass-made product from low-quality inputs—a pale imitation of, well, real beer, with little impact on the outcome of getting more dates.

Ask yourself: what is the real difference between a Whopper and a Big Mac? A Hummer and an Escalade? Pepsi and Coke? All offer slightly different flavors of the same perceived value. Perceived value, of course, isn't real value. It's imaginary! Differentiation is too often skin-deep. Words without meanings behind them—valid, accurate, and powerful economic meanings—lead inexorably to stuff that offers largely imaginary benefits. Imaginary benefits are the epitome of

148

thin value. That's the definition of and problem with meaningless business in a nutshell.

To be economically meaningful is to be able to *specify, prove,* and *improve* outcomes: "our customers get healthier"; "we make people fitter"; "our customers build stronger relationships"; "we make communities smarter." Outcomes that make a difference to well-being are what make our work meaningful. They are what make it matter in terms of authentic, thick value that accrues to people, communities, society, the natural world, and future generations.

Strategy in the seventies, eighties, and nineties was concerned with answering a fundamental question: what business are we really in? By answering this question in new ways, companies redefined their business models. Rolls-Royce and IBM shifted from products to services, for example, to capture value from installing, maintaining, and replacing those products. Today, that question cannot help us learn how to create thicker, more authentic value. In the twenty-first century, asking "what business are we really in" is obsolete, because it never asked us to create a fundamentally better *kind* of business in the first place.

Today, every company is in the same business: the *outcomes* business. The great challenge of the twenty-first century isn't deciding which flavor of meaningless, industrial age stuff to produce. It is learning to make stuff that's *not* meaningless stuff in the first place. It is learning how to make a lasting, tangible difference to well-being because that is the *only* foundation for the creation of authentic economic value.

How are today's radical innovators making their businesses meaningful? Through a radical new institution: *betters.* Twentieth-century businesses produce goods: products and services that offer us economic good or near-term utility. But goods are just outputs, and now all are in the outcomes business. Constructive capitalists are discovering that twenty-first-century businesses don't produce goods, they produce betters: bundles of products and services that make people, communities, society, the natural world, or future generations economically better by ensuring they achieve positive, tangible outcomes. At the outer limits, *betters* mean bundles of products and services that get better the *more* they're used—upending the industrial age precept that products and services must decay and dwindle as they're used.

You can think of betters as *what* transform outputs—the stuff the industrial era firm produces—to outcomes that enhance well-being. The more consistently and reliably we can transform outputs to better and better outcomes, the more economic effectiveness we have attained and the more of a difference we can make.

Just ask Nike. The twentieth-century Nike was obsessed with differentiation. It was a textbook brand orchestrator, push-marketing mass-produced athletic shoes, clothes, and accessories based on a new styles, colors, or technologies. Throughout the eighties and nineties, and well into the noughties, Nike was a company bereft of meaning. It was unconcerned with whether any of those outputs had a positive impact on people's outcomes. Its shoes might have helped you run better, they might have been expensive fashion accessories, or, worse, they might have been downright dangerous to your health. Christopher McDougall's book *Born to Run,* for example, discusses how "innovative" new running technologies helped lead to *higher* injury rates for an entire generation of runners by weakening foot and ankle muscles.[7]

The twenty-first-century Nike knows it's time to turn that upside down. It's obsessed not with differentiating stuff, but with making a difference. Today, it is disrupting the athletic industries yet again, this time, by producing betters. Nike Plus is its revolutionary online community, launched in 2006, where, according to *Wired,* "More than 1.2 million runners . . . have collectively tracked more than 130 million miles and burned more than 13 billion calories."[8] Nike Plus will, if you give it half a chance, work furiously to make you a better runner. There you can get expert coaching, set goals, create a running schedule, compete with other runners, track your runs, and trade running tips with others. Nike says Nike Plus is the world's largest running club, but it's much more than that. It's a turbocharged engine that boosts people's fitness, letting consumers get radically more health out of every run. *Betters* are about better: Nike's goal with Nike Plus is to help every customer become a better runner.

Simon Pestridge, Nike's marketing director in the United Kingdom, told *Revolution Magazine* about Nike's great shift from skin-deep differentiation to making a difference: "We're here to enable athletes to be even better." That focus on difference means, according to Pestridge, "We don't

do advertising any more. We just do cool stuff. It sounds a bit wanky, but that's just the way it is. Advertising is all about achieving awareness, and we no longer need awareness. We need to become part of people's lives."[9] Being part of people's lives means creating thick value that matters in human terms.

Roberto Tagliabue of Nike's Techlab, in an interview with innovation expert Sam Lawrence, explained that Nike Plus "is less about Nike and more about you, the athlete. Now the user is at the center and Nike is there to serve experiences to better them."[10] There's that key word again: *better*. Stefan Olander, Nike's vice president of digital sport, remarked in *Time* magazine, "In the past, the product was the end point of the consumer experience. Now it's the starting point."[11] Shoes are just a starting point: betters are what transform outputs to outcomes. Nike's thinking thick value.

Nike Plus, one of Nike's key growth platforms for the next decade, is built from the ground up to translate outputs—shoes—to tangible human outcomes by enhancing well-being. Rivals like Adidas and Puma are struggling because chasing more and more meaningless differentiation—less and less profitable, limited-edition, microtargeted sneakers in hundreds of different colorways that are then advertised furiously—is draining their businesses of profitability. Nike, on the other hand, is shedding differentiation's skin. In 1997, according to the *New York Times* and *Ad Age*, it spent 55 percent of its ad budget on traditional ads. By 2007, a year after Nike Plus's launch, that number was down to just 33 percent—a decline of over 50 percent.[12] Nike is investing less and less in the single biggest expenditure in its industry—traditional megamarketing—as part of a concerted effort to focus on initiatives like Nike Plus, where it sees a relatively greater return for every dollar it invests. Through those steeper returns, earned not by differentiation but by making a difference, Nike hopes to power another decade of historic growth.

Striving to make a difference instead of seeking differentiation upends orthodox competition. Many companies promise better outcomes that people *might* achieve. (Psst! Buy this toothpaste and the girlfriend or boyfriend of your dreams will fall into your arms!) Needless to say, it doesn't happen very often. The basis of competition hasn't really changed. Nike, in contrast, is altering the basis of competition in its industry. The new basis, because it yields greater returns, isn't glitzier marketing, broader distribution, or even more innovative products (they're just the starting point, remember?), but fitter customers—helping ensure that customers achieve better outcomes. *Ensuring* is the key word. Though they may promise a better relationship, neither Crest, Colgate, nor Aquafresh work to ensure one, but Nike Plus ensures better runs and running skills than Adidas or Puma. Instead of investing in differentiation, Nike is investing in difference. Instead of investing in traditional ads, Nike is investing in betters, because they redefine what it means to be competitive.

Betters transform outputs to outcomes by positively impacting one or more of four categories of well-being: physical, social, economic, and mental wellness. Here's what they

mean, and how constructive capitalists are making a difference to each.

Physical Wellness

In order to affect the category of physical wellness, you need to ask: Do we make people physically healthier and fitter, and help them live longer? Do we help them exercise regularly, diet properly, and rest fully? Do we help them maintain better hygiene and cleanliness?

For example, the well-being of consumers is the last thing on the minds of orthodox food retailers. They're concerned with moving product, and whether it's packed with preservatives or stuffed with saturated fat is of little importance. Caveat emptor: the nutrition information's on the label, and that's as much responsibility as we'll take, says Big Food.

Until Whole Foods came along. How did Whole Foods launch a revolution on an unsuspecting food industry? Simple, by focusing on physical well-being. Whole Foods built from scratch an organization focused not on product, but on the well-being of customers, on stocking and selling food that tasted better *and* made consumers healthier.

Whole Foods is far from perfect. For example, CEO John Mackey's infamous editorial in the *Wall Street Journal* objecting strenuously to a national health care plan and calling instead for further health care deregulation enraged customers and caused protests.[13] And, according to *Mother Jones* magazine, one of Whole Foods's own internal strategic goals is to be "100 percent union free."[14] It turns up the heat, intervening at the stirrings of collective action by employees and refusing to recognize unions even when workers do organize.

Yet, being constructive isn't about being perfect; it's about being better. Despite its many shortcomings, whatever its senior management's political leanings, what Whole Foods is committed to—that its industrial era rivals *aren't*—is the physical wellness of its customers. That commitment begins with a list of verboten ingredients, like artificial flavors and colors. It continues through a product range explicitly focused on improving health and a retail experience designed to help people make better food choices with better information about the origin and benefits of different products. It ends with in-store classes, workshops, and seminars about eating, drinking, and living better to maximize physical wellness.

Yesterday, Big Food saw Whole Foods as the peace-sign-waving hippie protesting outside the corporate boardroom. Today, Big Food is desperately playing catch up, imitating Whole Foods's innovations lock, stock, and barrel. Just ask Tesco, which has invested hundreds of millions in Fresh & Easy Neighborhood Market. But Whole Foods manages to consistently stay one step ahead of its imitators. Fresh & Easy, for example, has been a relative disappointment for Tesco, requiring significant marketing expenditures to kick-start meaningful growth. Why? Because imitators are too often faking it. If they don't have Whole Foods' policies, the actual food available in rivals' "healthy" stores might differ little in terms of ingredients, sourcing policies, and nutritional

content than what's available in their "unhealthy" stores. They haven't cottoned to Whole Foods' secret: despite its many flaws, it's not in the outputs business, and it never was. It is in the outcomes business, and what it strives to sell aren't goods, but betters. Every product, service, and store should enhance health, because food is just a means to the larger and more valuable end of physical wellness.

Social Wellness

Social wellness is about connectedness: the quality, intensity, durability, and quantity of relationships. To affect this category of wellness, you need to ask: Are we helping people have better relationships? Do we amplify the number of relationships people have? Do we facilitate more trusted relationships, with prolonged contact and more affiliation between people?

At the Sunrise Senior Living center in Edgbaston, United Kingdom, the chef lent his son's Wii to a staff member for the weekend, and a revolution was born. The *Independent* newspaper reported that seniors couldn't get enough of Wii Sports: "Bowling has proved to be the most popular game at the home where 90-year-old Barrie Edgar is emerging as a keen star. Mr Edgar said: 'It's fiercely competitive. We're all addicts and it's really bridged the generation gap.'"[15]

Feel-good fad? Think again. Sunrise Senior Living is an NYSE-traded company that operates more than four hundred senior care centers across the globe. Wiis are part and parcel of the daily life at most. Wiis were used at its center in good ole Alpharetta, Georgia, according to the *Atlanta Journal-Constitution:* "At a Sunrise Living residence in Alpharetta, the Wii Fit exercise program was used to turn the 3 p.m. social hour into a karaoke dance-off, with residents taking turns on the microphone to sing Frank Sinatra songs, and later following the steps for hip hop-inspired dance moves."[16]

Who would've imagined that video games could be a focal point for social interaction in families or for elderly people in care centers? Rivals like Sony and Microsoft didn't: they focused on more and more technically complex, graphics-heavy, meaningless games. In contrast, the Wii launched a social wellness revolution and redefined an entire industry. Yesterday, video games were activities teenage boys undertook in isolation. The Wii's goal was to make games fun for people again, to make video games focal points for social interaction among everyone, from goths to girls to grandparents. Wii Sports, Wii Play, Tetris Party, Rayman Raving Rabbids, Mario Kart, and Mario Party are all "party games." They are shared experiences whose goal is to enhance togetherness among people of all stripes. The Wii connected with Sunrise Senior Living for the same reason it broke new ground with frat houses, hard-core gamers, physical therapists, and just plain regular people. Wii games are more challenging, more fun, and more beneficial because they enhance social wellness. It's that razor-sharp focus on outcomes that helped Wii relegate PlayStation 3 and Xbox 360 to a distant second and third, building a vastly greater installed base at a pace that stunned Sony and Microsoft.

Here's a final vignette about Wii, courtesy of the *Denver Daily News*: "Eighty-seven-year-old Bill Alderson—representing the San Marino Strikers—said Wii Sports has allowed him to have fun again. He said he hasn't experienced this much joy since his wife Dixie passed away over three years ago."[17] Poignant—and powerful. Now *that's* positively affecting outcomes to create value that *matters*. How often do most industrial era companies make a difference like that even *once*, let alone consistently, as Nintendo does? Sadly, almost never.

Economic Wellness

Economic wellness is about helping others become more productive and efficient. In order to affect this category, you need to ask: Are our products and services usable? How effortlessly can people get the best outcomes out of them, every time they use them? Are we making people more secure against economic volatility and insecurity?

Economic wellness isn't about simply selling people low-priced goods and services, because they often simply lead to greater learning, maintenance, or replacement costs. The money you save by eating fast food for life, for example, will probably be counterbalanced by (ahem!) replacement costs of a pretty serious kind. Rather, economic wellness means, at an equivalent price, offering customers greater and longer-lasting gains.

Take, for example, Canon's Digital Learning Center. Learning to take great photographs is a mega-pain, and the jargon-filled manuals with most cameras are more harm than help. The process of becoming a better photographer usually involves thousands of photos, dozens of books, and lots of money. At the Digital Learning Center, you can browse technical help, tutorials, articles, and photos. It shows most of the photos with complete technical variables that the photographer used—aperture, focus, shutter speed, and the like. Through tutorial and technical help articles, you can also learn about why those variables are important, and how they affect the photos you take. You can register for Canon's Live Learning workshops and classes where you learn skills hands on. Canon's goal isn't just to sell more cameras, but, first, to make people productive photographers who get more out of every shot they take—a small but tangible kind of economic wellness that stays with people for life.

Perhaps the most radical example of economic wellness is Hindustan Unilever's Shakti initiative. Shakti's microloans empowered rural Indian women to become micro-entrepreneurs. The result was a powerful boost to economic wellness. Rural women were once at the mercy of the weather, their communities, and their husbands. Microloans and micro-entrepreneurship helped lift them out of economic insecurity, giving them the opportunity to earn a steady income and doubling their average incomes. That's new economic wellness where none existed before.

Mental Wellness

To address the category of mental wellness, you need to ask: Do we make people mentally healthier? Do we alleviate their anxiety, tension, and pressure? Do we make people mentally

fitter? Do we improve their thinking, reasoning, remembering, or judging skills?

Quick, what's the unlikeliest source of better mental fitness you can imagine? Here's a perfect candidate: video games, which, according to three decades worth of parents, make you stupid. When games in the 1980s consisted of shooting space invaders or, in the 1990s, zombies, they might have had a point.

But, not anymore. In addition to being a source of physical wellness, the Wii is a source of social wellness. It's just one front in Nintendo's war against meaningless business. Nintendo has pioneered the "brain games" genre across both its Wii and DS platforms. Games like Brain Age, Big Brain Academy, and Dr Kawashima's Brain Training give the young and the elderly alike better opportunities to exercise their mental muscles. While the academic jury's still out on whether brain games have a lasting impact on helping improve reasoning and memory skills, it's Nintendo's intent that counts: brain games are the living expression of Nintendo's focus on striving to have positive, tangible human outcome. And for Nintendo, the rewards for taking that step have been tremendous. Brain Age, Nintendo's biggest hit of recent years, has sold more copies than the number-one titles for the Xbox 360 and PlayStation 3 combined.

Zoom out, for a moment, to see the bigger picture behind Nintendo's revolution. Sony and Microsoft wanted the PlayStation 3 and Xbox 360 to be what the digerati call "digital lifestyle hubs"—places to hang out and consume more meaningless stuff that didn't matter. Nintendo, in contrast, wanted the Wii and Gameboy DS to be hubs for

betters—games that would make people tangibly and durably better off physically, socially, and mentally. Just five years
ago, after the costly failure of its GameCube, Nintendo's future was in doubt. Today, that relentless focus on being significantly more constructive than rivals is what has powered
Nintendo's dramatic reascension to the video games throne.
How far behind are Sony and Microsoft? It has sold nearly
as many Wiis as Microsoft and Sony have sold PlayStation 3s
and Xbox 360s—combined.

Summing Up

If, in a hypercompetitive world, where thousands of low-cost
producers can supply anything, anytime, anyplace, you're
still merely pursuing skin-deep differentiation—well, it's
game over. Twenty-first-century advantage demands redis-
covering what's meaningful and discarding what isn't. Some-
where out there is a company, a master of socio-effectiveness,
a creator of net happiness, a virtuoso of positive impact, that
can transform outputs to better outcomes—and render you
irrelevant. Unless you can make a difference, sooner or later
expect nothing but indifference from people, communities,
and society.

Here's a quick checklist, to kick-start your thinking. Ask
yourself:

- Like most, you're still probably still differentiating
  "product," to achieve superficial variation within
  a homogeneous universe of largely similar substi-

tutes. Go deeper: what's your impact? What kinds of out*comes* do your out*puts* lead to—positive or negative? Do the products or services you produce have an effect on the well-being of people, communities, society, or future generations? Is what you're doing meaningful, in real economic terms?

- What outcomes could and *should* your outputs produce? On what categories of well-being *should* you be having a positive impact? What kinds of well-being are the scarcest—and by implication, the most valuable—when you take a close, intimate look at the day-to-day lives your customers actually live?

- How can you help ensure that everyone achieves tangible, positive outcomes? How can you make a difference to every buyer, supplier, and customer?

- What kind of betters—bundles of supporting, nurturing products and services—can you imagine producing, to transform raw, inert outputs into outcomes? What would translate *stuff* into positive, enduring, meaningful *impact*?

Chapter Seven

Step Six: Constructive Strategy

From Dumb Growth to Smart Growth

SO YOU'RE A twenty-first-century business. Linear value chains? Forget it. You (re)produce in circular value cycles. You don't dictate value propositions; you hold value conversations. Your first principles of value creation are written into a concise philosophy. Perfection—not protection—is the end you seek. And you don't produce inert, raw goods; you make betters.

Congratulations, you've weathered the climb. Welcome to the apex. Institutions are cornerstones. Economics are the foundations built atop them. But the capstone of capitalism is growth. That's it for mastering the new sources of advantage and the cornerstones they rest upon. The sixth step in

becoming a constructive capitalist—*crafting a constructive strategy*—is the final touch in toppling the industrial era status quo: learning to carve a new capstone.

. . .

At the very beginning of this book, I discussed the legacy of the great crisis of the noughties. Not banks, bonuses, or bailouts, but cornerstones. The institutional cornerstones of industrial era capitalism are straining to support an authentic prosperity. Instead, diminishing returns at the highest macroeconomic level have been reached. Examined carefully, growth—itself a flawed measure of prosperity—has been consistently and reliably slowing, not just over the last half-decade, but over the last half-century. Yesterday's growth model has reached its limits; prosperity is waning and weakening, buckling and breaking.

It's counterintuitive: why has growth fallen into decline as industrial era capitalism has spread across the globe? After all, growth—the ability to power increased plenitude—is what makes capitalism superior to the kinds of economic organization that preceded or challenged it, whether socialism, feudalism, or mercantilism. It's what makes capitalism historically unique, desirable to society, and powerful for people.

Here's the catch: not all growth is created equal. Bernie Madoff grew an investment fund for decades, before that growth was revealed as a Ponzi scheme. In the sixteenth century, Spain discovered a mountain of silver in Peru, and instead of investing it, simply stamped millions of coins with it. The result was a quick burst of inflationary growth and two centuries of stagnation. Saudi Arabia has an ocean of oil, but has failed to build a single world-class university, financial institution, or high-skills industry. Is its growth likely to outlive its oil wealth? The lesson is that some kinds of growth are worth more than others.

Industrial era growth is, I humbly suggest, "dumb." It is growth that is ultimately (not just environmentally) unsustainable because it is locally, globally, and economically self-destructive. Respectively, it requires the poor to subsidize the rich, so the rich can consume more and more ephemeral, transient stuff, produced through industrial age diminishing-returns economics. Those are the inevitable results of the intensifying pursuit of thin value at global scale. Legendary bond maven, PIMCO's Bill Gross, explained dumb growth this way: once upon a time, "we were getting richer by making things, not paper." But for the last several decades, instead, "we, in effect, were hollowing out our productive future at the expense of worthless paper such as subprimes, dotcoms, or in part, blue chip stocks."[1] That's the very opposite of smart.

The three facets of dumb growth are the three new strategic challenges that twenty-first-century capitalism—and twenty-first-century capitalists—must answer. Today, companies can no longer prosper merely by selling toxic, diminishing-returns products to the rich, subsidized by the poor, because it is increasingly self-destructive for people, communities, society, the natural world, and future generations. The new macroeconomic environment of the twenty-

first century is a crueler mistress than that of the twentieth. Industrial era capitalism's definition of prosperity wasn't built to last. I'd like to suggest it might just be time to redefine prosperity and growth for the twenty-first century. If I had to sketch the barest outlines of such a definition, here's how I'd put it: smart growth by increasing returns to investment in the least well-off beats dumb growth by diminishing returns to consumption from the most well-off.

Where industrial era dumb growth is the growth of thin, low-quality value, "smart" growth is the growth of thick, high-quality value. Think of a creek overflowing versus the Hoover Dam bursting: that's the difference between the growth of thin and thick value. Smart growth happens when savings (not overconsumption) drive investment by the most well-off in the least well-off (instead of capital flowing vice versa), in assets governed by the network logic of increasing returns (instead of in diminishing-returns assets, like factories, combustion engines, and fast food).

Companies that can achieve smart growth climb to the apex of twenty-first-century economics: they construct the tallest, strongest foundations of advantage atop the new cornerstones that I've been discussing. Yesterday, Nike, Google, Walmart, and Apple were powered by dumb growth. Today, all are beginning to be powered by smart growth—never perfectly, totally, or absolutely; but enough, it seems, so they can break through to a new level of outperformance. Their example reveals what's "smart" about smart growth. Because it's built on a stronger kind of value, more resistant to crash and collapse, smart growth is tougher, longer-lasting, and worth more to people, communities, society, and future generations. That's what Adidas, Yahoo!, Target, Gap, and Sony—all rivals still pursuing dumb growth—are discovering the hard way.

Constructive strategy is the art of redrawing the boundaries of prosperity by turning *dumb growth smart*. Industrial era capitalists have competitive strategies; their common goal is to maximize the growth of shareholder value. Constructive capitalists have *constructive strategies* instead. Their goal? To maximize the growth of thick value, and so ignite smart growth.

A constructive strategy defines how an organization will achieve competitive outperformance by becoming radically more *useful* to people, communities, society, and future generations than rivals. The result of every successful constructive strategy is a tectonic, status-quo-shattering not just in the quantity of growth, but in the quality of growth.

Successful constructive strategies happen by applying the new sources of advantage for maximum effect: to erase the largest amounts of economic harm. Its grandmasters achieve victory by creating the largest amounts of *highest-quality* value, realizing the most constructive advantage, and powering the *smartest* growth.

The Game Board

So how can you start crafting a constructive strategy of your own? By using the constructive capitalism game board (see

FIGURE 7-1

The constructive capitalist game board

Thicker marginal value

		Locally smart growth	Globally smart growth	Economically smart growth
Difference	**Consciousness Epiphany**			Nike, Apple, Better Place, Nintendo
	Truth		Whole Foods	Walmart
Creativity	**Independence**		Shakti	
	Compassion		Starbucks	
Resilience	**Generosity**			Lego
	Leveling			Google
Responsive-ness	**Empowerment**	Findthefarmer, Jelli		
	Purpose	Threadless		
	Togetherness	Le Labo		
Loss advantage	**Endurance**	Interface		

Constructive strikes

Competitive arenas

figure 7-1). It's a flexible tool that can be used in many ways. I've built it to bring the *practice* of being a next-generation capitalist—of leaping to the next level of advantage—to life. It's no magic wand, panacea, or silver bullet—but, as a map of next-generation strategy space, the game board just might help you think strategically about *how, where, and why to compete* in a radically altered twenty-first-century economic landscape. You can use it to map which of your immediate rivals are becoming next-generation competitors, and which aren't. You can track and monitor competitive moves emerging and gaining steam across industries. Or you can use it directly, to begin getting disruptively constructive yourself.

There are two stages to using the game board: (1) choosing a new competitive arena, making a concrete decision about where to compete; and (2) in your chosen arena, selecting a constructive strike—making a specific decision about *how* to compete most disruptively.

Let's explore each step in turn. And, remember, if you want to get *truly* disruptive, think actively about the shortcomings of your own company, industry, and sector while you read.

Choosing a Competitive Arena

On the *x* axis of the game board are three new arenas of facets of smart growth: locally smart growth, globally smart growth, and economically smart growth. And because smart growth is the goal all constructive strategies strive to achieve, they're also the three arenas of twenty-first-century competition, in roughly ascending order of potential value creation, with the most potent—economically constructive growth—at the right. If you're not competing in any of

them, welcome back to the twentieth century: you're living on borrowed time.

Here's what shapes competition in each arena and how to choose among them.

Locally Smart Growth

Dumb growth is locally self-destructive to people, communities, and countries—because it's not built on investment, but on overconsumption instead. America in the noughties was the apotheosis of locally self-destructive growth: consuming houses, cars, and gadgets ravenously, yet failing to invest in better education, health care, energy, transportation, factories, software, or food, the result—inevitably—was crisis. Too often, growth in the most developed countries simply meant consuming more and more today at the expense of seeding a better tomorrow.

Where twentieth-century growth was built on consumption, twenty-first-century growth is built on investment. Being locally constructive means fueling people and communities investing in themselves, literally locally, instead of merely consuming more and more disposable—and ultimately self-destructive—stuff.

Yesterday, India's poor had to spend money daily on privately run, disproportionately expensive, and poorly regulated minibuses. They were forced to make ad hoc expenditures on transportation. Today, they can invest in a Nano. A car is an asset, an investment—one that depreciates, can be sold, and lives on a household's balance sheet. Yesterday, multinationals sold stuff to Indians. Today, the Shakti initiative helps poor, rural Indians invest in themselves by providing them with microloans, inventory, and entrepreneurial training—so they can become micro-entrepreneurs, with their own personal balance sheets. Both are textbook examples of locally constructive growth.

To become locally constructive, ask yourself: Are we fueling investment in people and communities, instead of consumption by them? Is what we sell an investment that people and communities can make in themselves—and if it's not, how can we make it one?

how do I do this?

Globally Smart Growth

Dumb growth is globally self-destructive across countries, societies, and continents—because it requires the poor to subsidize and leverage the rich. Under its terms, capital flows backward: *from* emerging markets, like China and India, *to* developed countries, like the United States and United Kingdom, to prop up overconsumption of the ever-more ephemeral. Developing nations' growth comes to depend on overconsumption in developed nations, and developed nations' growth comes to depend on lending by developing nations. Yet that game of musical chairs, that cycle of codependence, cannot continue indefinitely—because developing nations are ultimately only recycling the dollars and pounds developed nations spend. But growth that asks the poor to

lend to the rich to prop up consumption starves both sides of meaningful investment. And so industrial age cornerstones are failing to support an authentically shared prosperity.

Globally constructive growth happens, instead, when the rich invest in the poor, so *both* can invest in tomorrow. Consider the difference in terms of the late twentieth century's favorite business model. Offshoring design, production, and maybe even service to the lowest-cost, poorest countries was every CEO's favorite move yesterday. The problem, of course, is that what income poorer countries generate is insecure, volatile, and must be lent back to rich countries to fuel the consumption driving growth in the *first* place, or else there will be no one to consume stuff. Endgame? Unemployment and skills crises in developed countries—and forgone plenitude in poor ones.

Twenty-first-century businesses seek, instead, to make *low-cost* producers into *thick-value* producers: they invest in them, with them, and for them. Why? Because when low-cost producers become thick-value producers, new net value has been created for the poor, and the global economy no longer has to rely on overconsumption in rich countries, leveraged by poor countries, to prop up a house of cards. Ultimately, only when *everyone* is sustainably better off does greater consumption and more even growth become sustainable.

Why is Starbucks investing heavily in Fair Trade, which pays a premium to commodity coffee prices? Because paying a premium gives low-cost coffee growers the opportunity to invest in themselves and perhaps become high-value coffee artisans who are, in turn, able to enjoy higher levels of consumption themselves. Capital begins (a mere trickle, to be sure—but a start) to durably flow from richer to poorer in Starbucks's new model, so the poor can help power—and enjoy—an authentically shared prosperity.

To become globally constructive, ask yourself: Is the ultimate—not just proximate—result of what we produce causing capital to flow from the rich to the poor, instead of vice versa? Are we investing in developing country suppliers or squeezing them? Are we helping them build skills and competencies that can make them durably better off or are we treating them as low-cost commodities? What are we doing to reverse the vicious cycle of lending from the poor to the rich?

Economically Smart Growth

Dumb growth is economically self-destructive because industrial era business was dominated by diminishing-returns economics: the *more* resources are utilized, the *less* valuable they become; the more intensely they depreciate. Factories and machinery get worn out. Intellectual property becomes obsolete. Ads quickly reach saturation point. Scale itself reaches diminishing returns: you can sell tons more widgets, but each widget is less profitable than the last. Consumption itself realizes steeply diminishing returns when weighed in terms of happiness.

That was yesterday. Today, radical innovators are building twenty-first-century business on the network economics

of increasing returns. The *more* resources are utilized, the *more* valuable they become; the more they *app*reciate. Being economically constructive happens when tired, creaking, industrial era diminishing returns are replaced by hypersustainable increasing returns.

Science fiction? It's becoming reality in Beaverton, Oregon. The better runners become by using Nike Plus, the faster they will wear out running shoes. The faster skilled runners wear out running shoes, the more they will benefit from Nike's consistent development of more technologically advanced and harder wearing running shoes. In the near future, the more intensively Nike can remanufacture those shoes, the lower its cost base. It is becoming a business powered by increasing returns to shoe usage, not just a business powered by diminishing returns to shoe production. Nike's is an *awesomely* twenty-first-century business design—one that marries hard, physical resources to the network logic of increasing returns.

Like Nike, Walmart is striving to build a twenty-first-century business on the network economics of increasing returns. When you buy goods and services from the constructive Walmart, they will benefit the environment. As the natural resources replenish themselves, they decrease in cost, letting Walmart lower prices further, giving you a great incentive to buy more goods and services from Walmart. Walmart's goal is to unlock a virtuous circle, where thicker value offers increasing returns That's the theory, of course— and Walmart's great real-world challenge over the next decade is figuring out how, by tuning its value cycle, to bring it roaring to life—yet, the deeper point is that, to get there, Walmart has first had to make a great mental leap, smartening up by *seeking* a smarter kind of growth.

To become economically constructive, ask yourself: Are we still dominated by the industrial era economics of diminishing returns? How can we shift to the network economics of increasing returns? How can our products, services, or resources get better the *more* they are utilized?

Which of the new arenas of competition are you competing in? Are you competing for locally, globally, or, the most powerful, economically smart growth?

Selecting a Constructive Strike

Every revolutionary needs stuff to revolutionize—stuff that's insufferably awful, terrible, and, well, *dumb*. The new sources of advantage are applied with maximum effect when they erase the largest, most intense, and longest-lasting amounts of economic harm. Disruption happens when construction erases maximum destruction: when new cornerstones are brought to places and spaces where borrowing benefits from or shifting costs to people, communities, and society is—yawn—just business as usual. Constructive strategy is most disruptive where there is a growing surplus of destruction, because that is where the most economic harm can be prevented and turned into authentic, meaningful, sustainable value instead. It is, in short, the art of turning the thinnest value into the thickest, so the dumbest growth smartens

up. Call it a new equation for economic insurgency: disruption is construction minus the destruction your fiercest rival inflicts on people, communities, society, and future generations.

On the constructive capitalist game board's *y* axis are, in ascending order of disruptive potential, eleven constructive strikes (see figure 7-1). At their heart are vital points. Think of them as the nervous system of thin value: they are places and spaces where industrial age cornerstones are creating the thinnest of value—and so they indicate where the thickest *marginal* value can be created. Each constructive strike is a different way to begin overthrowing the drab dogma of the industrial age, by thickening up thin value into the economic equivalent of a double-fudge triple-caramel sundae (extra cream) instead.

Just as aikido grand masters have gained proficiency in a repertoire of techniques that strike the vital points of their opponents' nervous systems, the game board's vital features deal the most competitive damage to industrial age rivals, because they home in directly on a rising surplus of deep debt. Fundamental alterations of the familiar, basic competitive choices that characterize industrial age rivalry—*togetherness*, for example, ain't your grandpa's competitive move—these qualities are *how* to breach the bulwarks of dumb growth and turn it smart. Hence, constructive strikes can leave incumbents—whose businesses are often built on the nervous system of thin value—stunned, stumbling, or paralyzed, like a novice struck in the right place by an aikido master. Here's how they work, and how to begin making them yourself.

Endurance

Where is renewal most disruptive? In value chains dominated by disposability. The telltale sign is simple: frequent,
consistent, and systemic waste that's costly to dispose of,
indirectly or directly. In industries and markets where disposability is chronic, deep ownership—taking ownership of
goods and services past the point of disposal and across the
full value cycle—can dramatically alter how value is created
and to whom profits flow. Many companies will sell you razors, toothbrushes, sneakers, and furniture, but once you buy
them, they're yours forever. How many companies will take
ownership past the point of consumption? Almost none,
and that is why reversing disposability is such a powerful
path to rethinking strategy. Interface attacked disposability
with its pioneering ReEntry program, and Nike is planning
to do the same by remanufacturing shoes. Both have gleaned
the insight that, in rivals' value chains, resources will decay,
only to be bought again. But in value cycles, the same pool
of resources can persist, persevere, and endure. Now that's
smart. So wherever you see disposability—reverse it, and
seek endurance instead.

[handwritten margin note: What does this mean in GE context? How must we must amplify!]

Togetherness

Where else is renewal powerful? Wherever steps in production and consumption are fragmented across large distances.
Here are three giveaway signs: huge, energy-gulping lengths
between production and consumption, elaborate and costly
supply chain management, and chronic inventory risk. By

moving production and consumption as close in space and time as possible—getting hyperlocal—these industries can create new value. Consider perfume. Industrial era fragrances are still made in factories. Le Labo, a radical fragrance innovator, will cook up fresh batches for you in-store, remixing and blending ingredients right under your nose. The advantage? You get fresher, more intense fragrances that offer more authentic, sustainable benefits. Le Labo carries less inventory, realizes less risk, and creates less waste. Togetherness means bringing consumption and production closer. When a company masters it, as Le Labo is beginning to do, the result is thicker value growing smarter. So wherever you see a yawning chasm between production and consumption, buyers and suppliers—bridge the gap, and seek togetherness instead.

Purpose

Where is democracy most disruptive? Wherever there's a clear lack of responsiveness. In many industries, players seem incapable of making *any* decisions in the first place. They're like zombies, tottering shiftlessly and aimlessly toward the next quarter, season, or financial year, with little intent or purpose. Zombified industries have four telltale signals: a glacial pace of innovation and a lack of new ideas; apathetic customers; dwindling brand equity; and increased marketing investment. Consider the Gap, a business that, for the better part of a decade, has struggled to simply make appealing clothes. It churns out the same old, same old endlessly, while profitability continues to evaporate. Like a zombie, the Gap has lost the smarts to judge: it can't identify tomorrow's fashion today. But Threadless can effortlessly and instantaneously respond to the shifts in supply and demand that leave the Gap confused and frozen. Through the power of democracy, Threadless is dezombifying a paralyzed, braindead industry, bringing it roaring back to responsive, purposive life. That's smart growth: instead of purposelessly, repetitively mass-producing stuff to be discounted, Threadless is purposively fueling gains that matter more to people, communities, and society. So wherever you see zombies, don't reach for your pistol—build a pulpit, and start seeding a democracy instead.

Empowerment

Where else is democracy powerful? Wherever people, communities, and societies are economically harmed by managerial decisions, but are actively and consistently disempowered to affect them back. Here are three telltale signs of disempowerment: consumer apathy, frustration, or resistance; outsized lobbying and marketing expenditure; and elaborate corporate governance mechanisms like poison pills. Nowhere was disempowerment rifer than in music, where consumers were actively disempowered by a record industry that consistently gamed the charts, payola-ed its way onto the airwaves, and sued consumers when they revolted. Radiohead began clearing the cobwebs from this dungeon of disempowerment by letting consumers name their

own prices. New services like Jelli, Last.fm, Pandora, and, of course, iTunes are turning the industry on its head, empowering music fans by democratizing music consumption. The result? More and more artists are deciding they don't need labels at all. Just ask Madonna and U2, who have eschewed record labels entirely in favor of Live Nation, a concert promoter. So wherever you find disempowerment—seed a deep democracy instead.

Leveling

Where is resilience most disruptive? There's no clearer indicator of a lack of resilience than a playing field that's been tilted, because it says, "We can't compete on our own merits." In those industries and markets, fairness can turn dumb economics smart. Here are four telltale signs of a structurally tilted playing field: ongoing, costly litigation; innovations never brought to market; a lack of consumer choice; and squeeze effects, where buyers or suppliers are consistently driven out of business. Media are a textbook example: an industry dependent on side payments between advertisers and publishers, the bundling and tying of content to irrelevant ads, and the soft fixing of ad and content prices—all forms of unfair advantage. Google's principles are weapons of mass construction precisely because they began to annihilate this unethical behavior, giving audiences, artists, and advertisers alike a better, fairer alternative. Google's ongoing advantage depends on always doing so. The lesson? A dollar of growth generated from a tilted playing field is almost always counterbalanced by a nickel, dime, quarter, or more of harm. An evolutionary edge, and the smart growth it powers, happens only on even playing fields, so when you find a tilted one, level it.

Generosity ~~ambush?~~

Another arena in which resilience is disruptive is wherever players are hoarding resources. There are three telltale hoarding strategies. Sometimes, as in software, biotech, and nanotech, players build patent thickets, portfolios of patents that go unused because their purpose is to block rival patents. Sometimes, as in food retailing, players build land banks—portfolios of unused real estate—to exclude and deter rivals from acquiring prime locations. Sometimes, players hoard relationships to exclude players from acquiring key clients, as in finance, where banks offer preferential rates, discounts, and services. In the toy industry, companies hoard, catalog, and jealously guard designs, trademarks, and characters, long after they're commoditized and obsolete. Here's what they're all implicitly saying: "We can't evolve better stuff, so we're stockpiling yesterday's stuff, trying to corner the market."

The Lego Factory turned hoarding on its head. Instead of hoarding designs, Lego has open-sourced them, making them common property. The result? Lego has to invest less in eking out the last fading returns from old designs, because Lego users and the Lego Ambassadors program are always designing new sets and helping spark new ideas. Generosity

means trading, selling, licensing, or possibly even *sharing* what is hoarded, as Lego has done, so better stuff can evolve, unlocking smarter growth. So wherever you find hoarding, turn the tables and get generous instead: your evolutionary edge will thank you for it.

Compassion

Where is building a more complete market valuable? In many value chains, the squeeze is the order of the day: by squeezing buyers and suppliers, companies boost margins. But they rarely create authentic value. The flipside of a squeeze is that innovative capacity is destroyed across the value chain. When you can't invest in people, production, or processes, you can't create new markets, industries, and categories. The telltale signs are clear: suppliers and buyers constantly struggling, a tepid pace of innovation, and poor working conditions for those furthest upstream or downstream. In these value chains, there's nothing more revolutionary than turning the squeeze inside out, with compassion—a premium that others can use to invest in themselves, expanding the pie for everyone.

Starbucks has mounted a furious attack on squeeze by making a commitment to source all the coffee it sells in the United Kingdom, Ireland, and, more recently, New Zealand from Fair Trade–certified suppliers. Perhaps it's easy to criticize—and my goal isn't to persuade you of Starbucks' nobility. Rather, it's to point out that the goal of that commitment is to help coffee producers invest in themselves, ultimately fueling different, better kinds of coffee that can create new categories of drinks and new segments of coffee drinkers. It's the beginning of smart growth, which must always reflect the personal growth of *people*, not just the volume of "product." So wherever and whenever there's a squeeze—try, to put competitors in the wrong, and innovation on the front burner, with compassion instead.

Independence

Another area in which completing markets is valuable is wherever people are increasingly economically vulnerable. What are the signs? Wherever volatility is rising, wages are flat-lining, household balance sheets are stagnant, and access to public services is limited. In such places and spaces, the potential to get creative and hatch new industries and markets is seriously disruptive. Smart growth can't ignite because people find almost *any* kind of investment impossible to make. Nowhere is this truer than for India's rural poor.

The Shakti initiative's microloans to poor, rural women are a vivid example of launching an assault on economic insecurity and turning dumb growth smart. Shakti participants don't just buy stuff; they build businesses and learn to earn regular incomes. As their insecurity has been obliterated—not completely, but significantly enough to change hardscrabble lives—a shared prosperity for Hindustan Unilever, villages, and villagers has grown. Smart growth isn't achieved when the incomes of people, communities,

or societies grow, but when their assets do as well, so they're more independent—free from dependence on dumb, consumption-driven growth. So wherever business as usual fails to enhance dignity, and lift people out of vulnerability— indeed, wherever it seems to achieve the very *opposite*—seek independence instead.

Truth

Where is meaning most disruptive? Many industries are concerned about counterfeits. But many seemingly real products *are* counterfeits. Meaning can be radically constructive in industries focused on faking it—on simulating key inputs or outputs.

There are three telltale signs of such industries: Fake people, like Gilly Hicks, whose portrait hangs in every store. Gilly is a counterfeit, a fictional character with a detailed fictional family history three generations deep, carefully crafted by Abercrombie & Fitch to appear to have been the creator of casual women's wear stores. Fake ingredients, like flavor enhancers, which fool people's bodies by adding taste, but no nutrition. And fake brands, like Häagen Dazs, which was cooked up in a boardroom in New Jersey merely to *sound* Swedish (talk about faking it, printed on early ice cream containers were maps of Scandinavia). Such industries focus on differentiating similar, commodity product: they are faking key inputs and outputs because they're unconcerned with making a meaningful difference to *outcomes*.

Whole Foods, in contrast, turned the food industry upside down by rejecting artificial colors and flavors. Whole

Foods, in the interest of better outcomes, built supermarkets that carried only real food. Imagine that. Smart growth is never built on counterfeits. It's always the result of the real thing. So wherever you see a counterfeit, no matter how finely-crafted—try countering it with a healthy, meaningful dose of truth instead.

Epiphany

Where else is meaning revolutionary? In industries and markets that don't just *simulate* inputs and outputs, but *dissimulate* outcomes. To dissimulate is to conceal. Many industries work to mask, hide, and bury negative outcomes, so people, communities, and society remain unaware of them. There are three telltale signs of such industries and markets: "aspirational" brands, outsized marketing expenditure driven by more and more complex segmentation, and lobbying to protect standards and requirements.

Perhaps the master dissimulators of the industrial era were the Detroit automakers. As late as the fourth quarter of 2008, the eve of its destruction, GM spent millions on lobbying against Corporate Average Fuel Economy (CAFE) standards, which effectively define the average miles per gallon all cars should meet. In fact, from 2001 to 2008, GM spent over $100 million lobbying to defeat more stringent CAFE standards, because the bulk of its revenues flowed from SUVs and trucks. GM's argument was, "Consumer choice is lost, drivers are less safe, and resources will be diverted from innovation." Talk about dissimulation: it was transparent to insiders and outsiders alike that GM and its

cousins were simply trying to hide the fact that since 1985, they had made almost no progress in voluntarily improving fuel-efficiency.

Radical innovators like Better Place have had an epiphany; they are upending Detroit's dissimulation by striving instead to create beneficial outcomes for people, communities, society, the natural world, and future generations. They are upsetting yesterday's automakers by building a renewably powered auto industry. Having an epiphany means reaching the (often-sudden) understanding that this industry is working night and day to mask, hide, and conceal negative outcomes—and that, by having better ones, it can be flanked, encircled, and attacked. It means upending the old logic, and, in its place, creating the new understanding that yesterday was dumb, but tomorrow will be smart. So wherever you sense dissimulation—reflect on an epiphany instead.

Consciousness

In many industries and markets, the obverse is true. It's not that incumbents hide negative outcomes, but that they're seemingly oblivious to having lasting, positive ones. In turn, obliviousness to better outcomes leads to alienated, tuned-out customers, buyers, and suppliers who have come to expect only the lowest common denominator. There are three giveaways of such industries: customer alienation, churn, and apathy; outsized marketing expenditures; and shrinking production, research, and innovation budgets. For a decade, video game publishers licensed megabrands—from sports leagues like FIFA and content producers like Marvel—so they could code a game once and make marginal improvements to it over and over. FIFA 2003 was followed by FIFA 2004, 2005, and 2006. The result? An industry bereft of creativity and innovation, and full of alienation. Consumers grew just as frustrated as developers grew just as frustrated as retailers. Inevitably, growth flat-lined.

Then Nintendo came to town. The Wii was revolutionary because Nintendo's focus on outcomes forced it to be radically innovative. Nintendo's revolution was to make meaningless games meaningful again. If you bought a Wii, its authentically creative games would help you get smarter, fitter, and healthier. It's the same revolution, ultimately, that Nike is promoting in footwear: answering alienation and disengagement with a laser-sharp focus on well-being. By being conscious of what's deeply, resonantly meaningful, and what's merely meaningless, both Nintendo and Nike are reaching the pinnacle of smart growth. So whenever you see neglect, disregard, or sheer obliviousness to better outcomes—be mindful, and get conscious of what it would take to have them instead.

Summing Up

Yesterday, prosperity's great question was: how much more value than your nearest rival could you, over time, create? Today, prosperity's great question is: compared with your

fiercest competitor, how much more *meaningful, authentic, enduring* value can you, over time, create? Because it's locally, globally, and economically unsustainable, the twentieth century's consumption-driven, debt-fuelled, diminishing-returns-based growth isn't fit for twenty-first-century prosperity. So instead of imitating a carcinoma's dumb growth, where thinner and thinner value multiplies self-destructively, a new generation of insurgents are striving, bit by bit, to surmount prosperity's challenge, by modeling the redwood's smarter growth: investment-driven, deep-debt-free, increasing-returns-based growth that creates thicker and thicker value.

The capstone of capitalism is growth, and once you've climbed to the apex of institutional innovation, the final step in becoming a twenty-first-century capitalist is carving a new capstone. Have you made the leap from a competitive strategy, which merely grows shareholder value, to a constructive strategy that seeds the growth of thick value? Are you just growing faster, harder, cheaper—or are you growing *smarter*? Here's a checklist.

- Which vital points of thin value are present in your industry, sector, or category? Which of the value-destructive moves identified in each constructive strike are your rivals, buyers, or suppliers making? Which are *you* making?

- Which are tiny gaps, and which are yawning chasms? Which lead to the creation of the greatest, deepest debt to people, communities, society, and fuure generations?

- Which constructive strikes will you aim at them? How will you thicken thin value? How will that thick value grow, turning dumb growth smart?

- If you don't do any of the above, are rivals likely to take the battle to you? When you look across the landscape at your immediate—and distant—competitors, who's likely to craft a constructive strategy, and who already *has* one?

Chapter Eight

Constructive Capitalism

"CAPITALISM," the great John Maynard Keynes once remarked, as he embarked, in the wake of the Great Depression, on the renegade journey that would turn economics upside down, "is not a success. It is not intelligent, it is not beautiful, it is not just, it is not virtuous—and it doesn't deliver the goods." But his next sentence was even more perceptive: "But when we wonder what to put in its place, we are extremely perplexed."[1] So here's my humble suggestion: it's time to replace it with a *better* kind of capitalism, that *is* intelligent, beautiful, just, virtuous—and that *does* deliver the goods. One built for the twenty-first century that's dawn-

ing over a deeply, irreversibly, radically interdependent world.

So here's my humble suggestion: twentieth-century capitalism doesn't fit twenty-first-century economics. And neither do twentieth-century capitalists. They're caught in a dilemma. The capitalists' dilemma says: the great challenge of the twenty-first century isn't in making, marketing, and selling the same old deep-debt-subsidized, consumption-driven, diminishing-returns "product" in slightly better ways. It is in learning, as constructive capitalists have done, to make stuff that's *not* all of the above in the first place. It is to profit *more* from *less* economic harm, instead of being trapped to profit only through more harm.

Today, the vast majority of firms seem caught in that dilemma. So how are a tiny handful of insurgents breaking free of it? I've discussed five cornerstones these institutional innovators are pioneering with you—but here's the deeper, perhaps more fundamental belief underpinning them: think bigger. Change the world radically for the better.

For constructive capitalists, business isn't merely a zero-sum game to be won. Rather, it is, as Twitter CEO Evan Williams remarked to me when revealing Twitter's nascent philosophy, "a force for good in the world."[2] It's a pivotal instrument to confront the multitude of challenges, tiny and towering, urgent and slow-burning, local and global, facing people, communities, society, and future generations in the twilight of industrial era capitalism. By laying down new institutional cornerstones, building stronger economic foundations atop them, and raising the capstone of smarter growth, insurgents are—never easily, sometimes haltingly, always imperfectly—changing the world for the better.

Williams's first principle resulted from the Twitter team relentlessly asking itself the toughest of questions: "Why are we *really* here?" And that's true for most of the revolutionaries we've discussed: the journey to constructive capitalism is almost always an answer to the tough, world-changing questions that the decline of industrial era capitalism begs. What good is an energy industry that destroys the atmosphere? What good is a media industry that, with relentlessly intrusive, ever-more pervasive ads, pollutes the infosphere? What good is production that consumes the natural world? What good are banks that catastrophically deplete the financial sphere? What good is a food industry that sparks an epidemic of obesity? What good is an apparel industry that produces insipid clothes in joyless, dreary working conditions? What good are athletic shoes that don't make people fitter? Google, Twitter, Walmart, Banco Compartamos, Apple, Grameen, Whole Foods, Threadless, and Nike all say, "We can do better." None of these companies is perfect. They're *better.* Here's what their revolution says: Better is better. Better—for people, communities, society, the natural world, and future generations—is better for boardrooms and shareholders.

Allow me to put that in context. In the twentieth century, *worse* was often *better.* What was better for the bottom line was—perhaps not immediately, absolutely, or deliberately,

but often, ultimately, and sometimes unwittingly—worse for people, communities, and society. Twentieth-century capitalists tended to build worse-is-better businesses, engines of artificial, unsustainable, meaningless, thin value. That's the essence of the capitalist's dilemma.

In the twenty-first century, *better* is *better*. Today, the tables are turning. In an interdependent world, the contours of supply and demand are being reshaped: investors, buyers, suppliers, governments, and customers are all beginning to reward those who are free of deep debt (and, conversely, punish those who can profit only by overleveraging themselves on it), and so a better kind of business is *economically* better. What's better for people, communities, and society is already, and will continue to be, better for the bottom line. Twenty-first-century capitalists build better-is-better businesses.

Please note: I'm not suggesting that, having waved my wand, I have the "right" answer to this new calculus, or even that there is an easy "right" answer. What I *am* suggesting is that if you want to be a twenty-first-century capitalist, if you want to build stronger economic foundations, if you want to attain a higher level of advantage—well, then you've got to contend with this new calculus, and find *your* answer.

Better-is-better businesses create *thick value that lasts, matters, and grows*. Firms create thick value when they generate profits by activities that accrue benefits to (or absorb costs from) people, communities, and society, not solely to shareholders and boardrooms. Conversely, when businesses realize profit through harm—by action or inaction—to others, they have created thin value. Thick value is value that is more sustainable, meaningful, and authentic than that of rivals. Let me recap:

- *Sustainable value* is value that lasts beyond production and consumption. It doesn't fall apart like a house of cards every few years, quarters, or months. It isn't powered by the frothing of a bubble, but is driven by investment in tomorrow, replenishing what is taken and caring for what is seeded. When you think about it, only sustainable value can power a smarter kind of growth—because it is less vulnerable to sudden collapse and implosion. When you buy food that benefits the environment at a twenty-first-century Walmart, the value that is created for all endures long after you've eaten the food. When you learn to become a better runner at the twenty-first-century Nike, the value that is created stays with you long after you've worn out the shoes.

- *Meaningful value* is value that matters. It has a greater, more positive impact on people's outcomes (at an equal cost) in ways that matter most to them. Profitability can be gained by excluding and ultimately disempowering people—whether buyers, suppliers, competitors, or consumers—in order to limit and stifle rivalry. But having an impact on outcomes that matter to others depends instead on including and empowering them. Where the Gap's advantage depends on squeezing suppliers, Threadless's advantage

depends critically on including customers in product development, and empowering them to choose. Where Puma's advantage depends on excluding rivals from distribution channels and retailers, Nike's next-generation advantage depends on including runners and helping them learn—and helping them help *other* runners learn—how to run.

- *Authentic value* is value that grows; it benefits boardrooms, shareholders, people, communities, society, and the natural world. Competitive advantage is often selfish; it counterbalances the value businesses create for shareholders and boardrooms with costs to others. An advantage that fails to accrue to those outside the boardroom isn't economically valuable, because it cannot power a shared, growing prosperity built on others investing in their future. Constructive advantage, by contrast, creates authentic value that accrues to many or all. When Google plays fairly—in stark contrast to Microsoft's unfair play, which is repeatedly challenged by regulators—society and people are better off. When Nike helps customers become better runners and sells them recyclable shoes, people, communities, society, and the natural world are better off.

By creating thick value, institutional innovators are able to break through to the next level of advantage: constructive advantage. It is an advantage in the quantity *and* quality of profit. Instead of shifting costs to or borrowing benefits from people, communities, society, the natural world, and

future generations, constructive capitalists minimize economic harm and replace it with a loss advantage, turbocharged responsiveness, resilience, economic creativity, or most powerfully, a lasting difference to well-being.

What are the wellsprings of constructive advantage? The new cornerstones I've discussed with you—value cycles, value conversations, philosophies, perfection, and betters. On them, stronger, broader, more robust economic foundations can be built. Industrial age capitalists seek to achieve operating efficiency, strategic agility, operating effectiveness, and labor and capital productivity. What is maximized is low-quality profit, which is divorced from positive, tangible human impact. Low-quality profit creates thin, inauthentic value. Instead, twenty-first-century capitalists maximize socio-efficiency, socio-productivity, managerial agility, evolvability, and socio-effectiveness. What is maximized is high-quality profit, which reflects tangible, enduring gains enjoyed by people, communities, society, the natural world, and future generations. High-quality profit creates thick value—authentic, meaningful, sustainable economic value.

So "we can do better"—or, in Williams's words, "being" a force for good in the world—means that in the twenty-first century, superior amounts of higher-quality profitability happen when better is better and when thicker value has been created. Make no mistake: thick value isn't easy to create. It's brain-crushingly difficult, not for the faint of heart. Most companies run from its challenge like hapless campers do from grizzlies. What makes constructive capitalists different is that they've seen its promise, taken on its

challenge—and discovered how to answer it. Through a radical new set of institutional cornerstones, they are—sometimes slowly, often painfully, never absolutely, but *always* disruptively—bringing thick value roaring to life. If you're not following their lead, prepare to become about as necessary to the twenty-first century as, to paraphrase Gloria Steinem, a bicycle is to a fish.

Most businesses still conceive of superiority as being better than a cohort of immediate, familiar competitors. But thick value says that just being better than the next guy, the next ten guys, or the next hundred guys isn't good enough for competitive superiority in the twenty-first century. Constructive capitalists aren't merely seeking to be better than rivals in *yesterday's* terms. They are fundamentally redefining what success means, to encompass the well-being of people, communities, society, and future generations; to return what you might call profit "plus"; profit *plus* social, environmental, human, and as yet unknown—unexplored kinds of—returns.

So competitive superiority in the twenty-first century happens by building a better-is-better business, not merely a better-than business. Thicker, deep-debt-free value offers greater, less risky, more durable, more desirable, higher-quality profitability because each dollar of it is created without economic harm and reflects meaningful, enduring benefits. Hence, constructive capitalists aren't worth *less* than their industrial era counterparts, but usually, disruptively more.

The flipside of *better is better* is that *worse is worse*. Industrial era business is worse because it is economically worse.

That is, it's inefficient, unproductive, inflexible, and ineffective, in twenty-first-century terms, at creating value that matters, lasts, and grows; it's an engine of low-quality profit. So it is increasingly a poor bet for companies, managers, and investors, in the same way it has increasingly been, as diminishing returns to prosperity suggest, for people, communities, society, and future generations.

Consider the many companies I've discussed in this book. Apple and Nintendo have learned that creating "impossible" new markets and categories yields higher quality, less risky, more defensible, more enduring profit that attracts investors in droves and disrupts rivals like Sony and Nokia, whose intensifying battles over yesterday's dwindling, low-quality profit has led investors to steadily vanish. The Big Three lost more than $50 billion in 2008, and GM required a historic bailout. Though they may slowly recover minor-league advantage, contrast that with the waiting lists for Tata's Nano. Tata's higher-quality profit, which stems from being able to surf an untapped, surging tide of global demand, will likely grow faster and more durably than Detroit's automakers, whose addiction to yesterday's markets and categories (SUVs, I'm looking at you) cost them the future. Of course, if Tata wanted to raise the stakes to even *higher*-quality profit, it would, like Better Place, get out of the petroleum combustion engine business and into the renewably powered transportation business.

There's low—and then there's the ocean's deepest point, the Mariana Trench. In terms of quality, the bulk of Wall Street's profits are to be found there. They will likely continue

to be devalued by banking levies and taxes and a more challenging and intense risk: the risk that delinquency rates will spike, counterparties default, or depositors flee—key causes of the *next* meltdown central bankers and financial authorities are *already* discussing. Banco Compartamos's delinquency rate of less than 3 percent, then, might not last forever, and may well be susceptible to deterioration. But in the teeth of a global banking crisis, Compartamos already *has* higher-quality profitability. JPMorgan Chase notes that Compartamos's "very solid asset quality" yields more sustainable, smarter growth.[3]

Threadless is, according to my informal estimate, already more profitable than Gap, and (with apologies) that gap will likely only widen. This is not simply because Threadless enjoys lower production, marketing, and discounting costs—all subject to change in a volatile world—but, more deeply, because it prospers by making clothes that matter more to people, matching their preferences more closely: a less risky, less working-capital-intensive, more sustainable set of economics that reflects the smart growth of higher-quality profit. Google has grown to become disruptively more profitable than Yahoo! and AOL—not to mention most of big media put together—by providing fewer but more *relevant* ads: higher-quality profit, yielding smarter, more enduring growth. Walmart and Whole Foods, pursuing very different approaches to creating thicker value—the former focused on environmental wealth, the latter, on human health—find their higher-quality profit and smarter growth inexorably devaluing rivals like Target and Tesco. Nike's no paragon of perfection—yet, by slashing waste, cycling inputs, and focusing on outcomes, it has built a lower-cost, higher-margin business that requires less mega-marketing, less overhead, and smaller amounts of raw materials to earn greater returns for shareholders *and* stakeholders; and that higher quality profit is taking Adidas to the mat.

Construction *is* today's disruption. Sweeping across the economy, a new generation of renegades is carving new institutional cornerstones so they can surmount the towering challenges of twenty-first-century economics, and topple the tired, toxic status quo. The ambition of their insurrection? It might, just might, be worthy of being called an enlightenment: not just the repackaging of stuff or the reengineering of work, but the reconception of *worth*.

None of the companies I've just mentioned—not a single one—is a paragon of perfection, a master mason of today's and tomorrow's cornerstones. But these and many more innovators are just a few of the renegades creating a future where, because worse is worse, better is better. In each of their unfinished journeys lies a deeper promise—navigating past the depleted affluence of the industrial age, beyond the edge of the world of business as we know it, to reach the fertile shores of a revitalized prosperity.

It's the arc of that larger story, a voyage past the bounds of industrial age prosperity, that I hope you've traced with me. Cast your sight beyond *this* cast of characters to the thread that binds them—and that will bind tomorrow's as-yet-unforeseen players. In building better-is-better businesses, constructive capitalists aren't just outperforming their rivals—the real story is that constructive advantage is beginning to make those rivals obsolete. Zoom out: in the

bigger picture, I'd like to suggest that constructive capitalists, for all their very real imperfections, might just be improving capitalism's value equation of creative destruction. They're learning to *minimize* the losses from destruction and *maximize* the gains from creation. They tend to incur fewer, smaller, and less unfair losses from destruction while offering larger, more frequent, and broader gains from creation.

By hardwiring an interdependent world's often invisible, but very real, human, social, public, and environmental costs and benefits into the heart of management; by giving back the benefits that are borrowed from, and taking back the costs that are shifted to, people, communities, society, future generations, and the natural world; their new institutions are beginning to destroy *less,* to create *more.* Constructive capitalists are stepping toward a worthier capitalism: one that yields more authentic, sustainable, meaningful value for every dollar, rupee, or renminbi spent.

To survive and thrive, you must make the leap yourself. To be an institutional innovator means literally not just reading from an updated economic blueprint, but *writing* one. My goal hasn't been to write that new blueprint—but to give you pen, paper, and maybe even a handful of design elements, for writing your own.

If that task sounds daunting, then consider this: capitalism is neither descended from Mount Olympus, nor ordained by nature. It is one of *humanity's* great creations—embedded in our noisy, messy world. It's constructed anew every day, with every decision we make. Like every other human creation, it would be presumptuous to conclude that we've reached the final destination, the end of the line, the summit of the climb; that capitalism's astonishing, improbable journey finishes here.

Yet, because it's *lived*, the future of capitalism won't begin in essays, proclamations, regulations, headlines, articles, computer models, equations, or dusty tomes like this one. Perhaps that's because instead of wondering whether it actually is possible to make a quantum leap into an unexplored *terra nova* of prosperity, all the institutional innovators whose stories I've told are already too busy rolling up their sleeves and writing their own blueprints.

"What are the wellsprings, deep and true, of a more enduring, meaningful, authentic prosperity?' That's capitalism's great question. And for many years we've taken for granted that it has been answered. But the truth is that there probably *are* no eternal, simple answers to this great query—just better (and better) ones. Far from suggesting that I've offered you all (or even any) of those better answers, what I hope you've taken away from this book is this: the suggestion that it might just be time to—as each constructive capitalist has done—ask yourself that question anew.

The future of capitalism begins, in other words, with *you*. So don't just read this book. Use it. It's not a textbook; it's a handbook. The protectors of the past never create the future. And the creators of the future never stop questioning the past. You've got to ask—and keep asking.

Notes

Foreword

1. http://www.ft.com/indepth/capitalism-future.

Chapter 1

1. Simon Kuznets, "National Income, 1929–1932," 73rd US Congress, 2d session, Senate document no. 124, 1934, page 7.

2. U.S. Treasury Department, *Major Foreign Holders of Treasury Securities, Treasury International Capital System Statistics,* 2009.

3. Niall Ferguson, "The Great Repression: A Long Shadow," *Financial Times,* September 21, 2008; Kenneth Rogoff, "The Great Contraction of 2008–2009," *Project Syndicate,* November 2, 2009; and Robert Reich, "The Great Crash of 2008," December 1, 2008.

4. Quoted in Nathan Gardels, "Don't Expect Recovery Before 2012—with 8% Inflation," *New Perspectives Quarterly,* January 16, 2009.

5. See Alan Greenspan, speech to the Economic Club of New York, February 17, 2009; and Michael Hirsh, "The Re-education of Larry Summers," *Newsweek,* February 21, 2009.

6. Paul Krugman, from the Lionel Robbins Memorial Lectures, The London School of Economics, 2009; Paul Krugman "The Other-Worldly Philosophers", *The Economist,* July 16, 2009; Willem Buiter, "The Unfortunate Uselessness of Most 'State of the Art' Academic Monetary Economics," *Financial Times,* March 3, 2009; Jospeh Stiglitz, "Wall Street's Toxic Message," *Vanity Fair,* July 2009; Fareed Zakaria, "The Return of Capitalism," *Washington Post,* June 15, 2009.

7. Douglass C. North, "Economic Performance Through Time," prize lecture, Sveriges Riksbank Prize in Economic Sciences in Memory of Alfred Nobel, 1993; Daron Acemoglu, Simon Johnson, and James Robinson, "Institutions as the Fundamental Cause of Long Run Growth," manuscript prepared for *The Handbook of Economic Growth*, April 29, 2004.

8. Alfred D. Chandler Jr., with the assistance of Takashi Hikino, *Scale and Scope: The Dynamics of Industrial Capitalism* (Cambridge, MA: Belknap Press, 1994); Hyman P. Minsky, *Stabilizing an Unstable Economy* (New Haven: Yale University Press, 2008); Joseph A. Schumpeter, *Capitalism, Socialism, and Democracy* (New York, London: Harper & Brothers, 1942).

9. Nouriel Roubini, "The Shadow Banking System Is Unravelling," *Financial Times*, September 21, 2008.

10. James E. McWilliams, "Vegetarianism Is a Major Step for Environmental Change," *Washington Post*, November 16, 2009.

11. "The Real Price of Gasoline,"International Center for Technology Assessment, Washington, DC, November 1998.

12. Michael D. Bordo, "Growing Up to Financial Stability," NBER Working Paper 12993, March 2007.

13. Bryan Smith, Peter M. Senge, Sara Schley, Joe Laur, and Nina Kruschwitz, *The Necessary Revolution: How Individuals and Organizations Are Working Together to Create a Sustainable World* (New York: Broadway Books, June 2008).

14. David Held, Mary Kaldor, and Danny Quah, "The Hydra-Headed Crisis," *Global Policy Journal*, April 2010.

15. Jeffrey Sachs and Lisa D. Cook, "Regional Public Goods in International Assistance," in *Global Public Goods: International Cooperation in the 21st Century*, eds. Inge Kaul, Isabelle Grunberg, and Marc A. Stern (New York: Oxford University Press, 1999).

16. Jack Hirshleifer, "The Private and Social Value of Information and the Reward to Inventive Activity," *American Economic Review* 61, no. 4 (September 1971): 561–574.

17. John Hagel III and John Seely Brown, "The Case for Institutional Innovation," HBR.org, March 4, 2009.

18. Gary Hamel, *The Future of Management* (Boston: Harvard Business School Press, 2007).

19. Smith et al., *The Necessary Revolution.*

20. "Mobility Takes Center Stage: The 2010 Accenture Consumer Electronics Products and Services Usage Report," 2010.

Chapter 2

1. Bryan Smith, Peter M. Senge, Sara Schley, Joe Laur, and Nina Kruschwitz, *The Necessary Revolution: How Individuals and Organizations Are Working Together to Create a Sustainable World* (New York: Broadway Books, June 2008); Paul Hawken, Amory Lovins, and L. Hunter Lovins, *Natural Capitalism: Creating the Next Industrial Revolution* (Boston: Little Brown and Company, 1999); Joseph Stiglitz, Amartya Sen, and Jean-Paul Fitoussi, *Mismeasuring Our Lives: Why GDP Doesn't Add Up* (New York: The New Press, 2010).

2. Personal correspondence with Adam Werbach, April 17, 2010.

3. Nike Corporate Sustainability Report 2007–2009.

4. Nike Gamechangers Blog, January 27, 2009.

5. Nike Grind, mission statement at NikeReuseAShoe.com.

6. "Nature and the Industrial Enterprise," *Engineering Enterprise* (Spring 2004).

7. "Sustainable Growth—Interface Inc.," *Fast Company*, March 1998.

8. Interview with Ray C. Anderson, Altenergystocks.com, November 13, 2009.

Chapter 3

1. Personal correspondence with Jake Nickell, April 13, 2010.

2. Don Tapscott and Anthony D. Williams, *Wikinomics: How Mass Collaboration Changes Everything* (New York: Penguin USA, 2008); Stan Davis and Christopher Meyer, *Blur: The Speed of Change in the Connected Economy* (Reading, MA: Addison-Wesley, 1998).

3. Nickell, April 13, 2010.

4. http://www.jelli.net.

5. "User-Controlled 'Jelli' to Debut on Live 105," FMQB.com, June 17, 2009.

6. Jim Giles, "Internet Encyclopedias Go Head to Head," *Nature*, Special Report (December 2005).

7. http://en.wikipedia.org/wiki/Cloture.

Chapter 4

1. Interview with Brian Fitzpatrick, May 6, 2010.

Notes

Chapter 5

1. Eric M. Strauss, "Apples for Sale on New York City's Upper West Side," ABC News, November 13, 2009.

2. Emma Rothschild, "Can We Transform the Auto-Industrial Society?" *New York Review of Books*, February 26, 2009.

3. Ramon P. DeGennaro, "Market Imperfections," Working Paper 2005-12, Federal Reserve Bank of Atlanta Working Paper Series, July 2005.

4. Chuck Squatriglia, "Better Place Unveils an Electric Car Battery Swap Station," *Autopia*, May 13, 2009.

5. Gavin Neath and Vijay Sharma, "The Shakti Revolution," Development Outreach, the World Bank Institute, June 2008.

Chapter 6

1. See, for example: National Opinion Research Center, General Social Survey, 2008; Japanese Cabinet Office, National Survey on Lifestyle Preferences, 2006. Kaare Christensen, Anne Maria Herskind, and James W. Vaupel, "Why Danes Are Smug: Comparative Study of Life Satisfaction in the European Union," *British Medical Journal*, December 23, 2006.

2. Richard Easterlin and Laura Angelescu, "Happiness and Growth the World Over: Time Series Evidence on the Happiness-Income Paradox," IZA Discussion Paper 4060, March 2009.

3. Richard Layard, "Happiness: Has Social Science a Clue?" Lionel Robbins Memorial Lectures 2002/3, London School of Economics, March 3, 2003.

4. B. Joseph Pine and James H. Gilmore, *The Experience Economy: Work Is Theater & Every Business a Stage* (Boston: Harvard Business School Press, 1999).

5. Michael Hammer and James Champy, *Reengineering the Corporation: A Manifesto for Business Revolution* (Sydney: Allen & Unwin, 1994).

6. Al Ries and Jack Trout, *Positioning: The Battle for Your Mind* (New York: McGraw Hill, 2000).

7. Christopher McDougall, *Born to Run: A Hidden Tribe, Superathletes, and the Greatest Race the World Has Never Seen* (New York: Knopf, 2009).

8. Mark McClusky, "The Nike Experiment: How the Shoe Giant Unleashed the Power of Personal Metrics," *Wired*, June 22, 2009.

9. Gareth Jones, "Nike: Just Do Digital," *Revolution*, January 9, 2009.

10. Gobigalways.com, April 30, 2008.

11. Sean Gregory, "Cool Runnings," *Time*, October 4, 2007.

12. Louise Story, "The New Advertising Outlet: Your Life," *New York Times*, October 14, 2007.

13. John Mackey, "The Whole Foods Alternative to Obamacare," *Wall Street Journal*, August 11, 2009.

14. Josh Harkinson, "Are Starbucks and Whole Foods Union Busters?" *Mother Jones*, April 6, 2009.

15. Sophie Borland, "Elderly 'Addicted' to Nintendo Wii at Care Home," *Telegraph*, September 14, 2007.

16. Helena Oliveiro, "Seniors Find Wii a Winner," *Atlanta Journal-Constitution*, April 26, 2009.

17. Peter Marcus, "Seniors Enjoy a Little 'Wii-Hab,'" *Denver Daily News*, June 12, 2008.

Chapter 7

1. Bill Gross, "Midnight Candles," *Investment Outlook*, November 2009.

Chapter 8

1. John Maynard Keynes, "National Self-Sufficiency," *The Yale Review*, vol 22, no. 4 (June 1933).

2. Interview with Evan Williams, Austin, Texas, March 2010.

3. Juan M. Partida and Frederic de Mariz, JP Morgan, Latin America Equity Research, "Banco Compartamos: Market Leadership Sustained by Superior Efficiency," April 29, 2008.

Index

Index

Index

Index

Index

About the Author

Umair Haque is the Director of the Havas Media Lab, a global research institute based in London, New York, and Barcelona. Prior to the Lab, he founded Bubblegeneration, an agenda-setting advisory boutique that counseled top-tier investors, start-ups, and corporations, and worked as a banker, trader, and strategy consultant. He studied Neuroscience at McGill University and received an MBA from London Business School, where he did research with Gary Hamel. He is a longtime blogger at HBR.org, and has been published or interviewed by *Wired*, *The Red Herring*, *BusinessWeek*, *The Globe and Mail*, and *The Guardian*.